3

Story & Art by

Taeko Watanabe

Contents

Story Thus Far

It is the end of the Bakumatsu era, in the third year of Bunkyu (1863), in Kyoto. The Mibu-Roshi (later to become the Shinsengumi) is created to protect the shogun in this chaotic time.

Both Tominaga Sei's father and brother are killed by anti-Shogunate rebels. Sei then joins the Mibu-Roshi Party disguised as a boy with the name Kamiya Seizaburo to avenge her family. She comes to regard Okita Soji as her mentor after he saves her from being attacked. Sei aspires to become a true bushi, but she finds herself surrounded by "animals." Further, Soji soon discovers Sei is a girl. Soji agrees to keep her secret after she tells him her tragic story. He looks after Sei in the Mibu-Roshi, and she finds herself starting to have feelings for him.

Sei finds her family's foe, and although it is in the form of suicide, retribution for the deaths of Sei's father and brother is achieved. The incident leads her to discover the spirit of the samurai in protecting the one she loves, but...

Characters

Tominaga Sei
She disguises herself as a boy to enter the Mibu-Roshi. Sei wants to become a warrior so she can avenge her father and brother. She trains under Soji, aspiring to become a true bushi.

Okita Soji
Assistant vice captain of the Mibu-Roshi and the selected successor of the Ten'nen Rishin-ryu school of sword fighting. He is the only member of the Mibu-Roshi who knows Sei's secret.

Saito Hajime
Assistant vice captain. He was a friend of Sei's older brother, Yuma, to whom he bears a striking resemblance.

Akesato
A Shimabara prostitute. She was Sei's late brother's lover, and someone who knows Sei's true identity.

Serizawa Kamo
Captain of the Mibu-Roshi. Captain Serizawa of the Mito clan has a lackadaisical—and often inebriated—facade that belies his cunning and calculating mind.

Hijikata Toshizo
Vice captain of the Mibu-Roshi. He commands the Mibu-Roshi with strict authority.

Kondo Isami
Captain of the Mibu-Roshi and fourth master of the Ten'nen Rishin-ryu. Has a very calm temperament and is highly respected.

SUMMER OF THE THIRD YEAR OF BUNKYU (1863)...

THE MIBU-ROSHI RESIDENCE UNDER LORD MATSUDAIRA OF HIGO, THE PROTECTOR OF KYOTO.

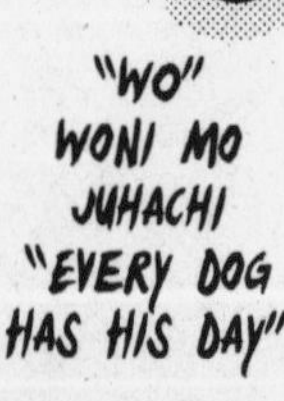

"WO"
WONI MO JUHACHI
"EVERY DOG HAS HIS DAY"

KYOTO "IROHA" KARUTA GAME

TIP-TOE
SHIP
I GOT YOU!!
ZZZ

WUMP
Ah.
YOU CROOK!!
SLAM
OUWWWWW!
Ugh...
DAMN IT.
I ALMOST HAD YOU.
...KAMIYA-SAN...
OH.
GOOD MORNING, OKITA-SENSEI!

EXCUSE MY RUDE ENTRY, SAITO-SENSEI.

IT'S TIME TO GET UP, SO PLEASE GET READY.

still half asleep

ROOMIES

GETTING UP IS FINE, BUT...

IS THERE ANY WAY THAT YOU CAN GET ME UP A LITTLE MORE GENTLY, KAMIYA-SAN?

I'M BESIDE MYSELF WITH FEAR SINCE YOU'VE BEEN TRYING TO SCORE A HIT OFF OF ME DAY OR NIGHT.

YOU SAY THAT, BUT I CAN'T EVEN BRUSH YOU WITH MY SWORD.
MASTER SWORDSMAN AND SELECTED SUCCESSOR OF TEN'NEN RISHIN-RYU, OKITA SOJI, FUJIWARA KANEYOSHI-SENSEI, I AM IMPRESSED!

KAMIYA SEIZABURO...

HOPES THAT, WITH DAILY DEVOTION, ONE DAY HE WILL BE WORTHY OF YOUR GREATNESS.

I BEG YOU TO PLEASE EXCUSE MY BREACH OF ETIQUETTE FOR THE TIME BEING.

YES, OSAKA ...

IN THE MIDST OF A BRAWL WITH THE ABLE SWORDS-MEN...

I, SEIZABURO, REALIZED...
THAT THERE WAS SOME-THING THAT I WANTED TO PROTECT, EVEN IF IT COST MY LIFE.

FOR THAT, IT WOULD BE AN HONOR TO BE CALLED AN *ONI*.
SPLASH
NOW I WANT THE STRENGTH TO PROTECT MORE THAN ANYTHING ...
DAMN IT...
YOU STILL WANT TO CONTINUE?
OF COURSE!!
YEAH KAMIYA!
GO, GO!
EYYYY!
S-BAP
S-BAP
S-BAP
S-BAP
HUP.

BAM
TSUKI! KAMIYA WINS!
WAAAA
WOW ...
—TOOK ONE FROM SANO!
THEY CHANGE ONCE THEY EXPERIENCE A BLOODY BATTLE.
HE'S GOING TO REALLY IMPROVE, SOJI.
HARADA-SAN'S SPECIALTY IS THE SPEAR.
HE'S NOT VERY GOOD WITH THE KATANA.
YEAH!
YEAH!
That was really something Kamiya!

WHAT?
IT'S NOT LIKE YOU TO SAY THINGS LIKE THAT.
DO YOU THINK SO?
I'M REALLY NOT AS NICE AS YOU, HIJIKATA-SAN.

You little rascal!
Let me kiss you!
Harada-san, what kind of logic is that!?
KAMIYA-SAN, COME HERE!

YES, OKITA-SENSEI!

ARE YOU SO PROUD THAT YOU WERE ABLE TO TAKE A HIT OFF OF HIM AFTER HE *ENTERTAINED* YOU FIVE TIMES?
IF THIS WERE A REAL BATTLE, YOU WOULD HAVE ALREADY BEEN DEAD FOUR TIMES OVER.

...!

I'M... SORRY.
I HAVE TO TALK TO YOU. FOLLOW ME.
YES...
VSH
EYYY!
SMACK

BAM
...HE HE HE...
YOU REALLY NEVER LET YOUR GUARD DOWN.
LEAVE THE MIBU-ROSHI, KAMIYA-SAN.

WHAT?
THIS IS NO PLACE FOR A GIRL.

I'VE LOOKED THE OTHER WAY SO YOU COULD AVENGE YOUR FAMILY.
BUT, NOW THAT YOU'VE ACCOMPLISHED THAT, YOU SHOULDN'T HAVE ANY REASON TO STAY.

I DO!!

I WANT TO SERVE MY COUNTRY WITH ALL THE OTHER SENSEI!

I AM NOT A GIRL! I'M BUSHI!

PLEASE LET ME STAY—PLEASE!!

YOU WILL ONLY GET IN THE WAY.

!

I WILL SPEAK TO THE CAPTAINS.

WELL ...

WHAT IF I GET JUST ONE HIT OFF OF YOU? JUST ONE!

YOU CAN'T SAY THAT I'D GET IN YOUR WAY, RIGHT?!

HUH?
PLEASE GIVE ME A CHANCE!!
IF I CAN SUCCESSFULLY SCORE A POINT OFF OF YOU LIKE IN KENDO— JUST ONCE IN THE NEXT THREE DAYS— YOU MUST ACCEPT ME AS A MAN!

AND, IF I FAIL...
I WILL LEAVE THE MIBU-ROSHI!

THE DEADLINE IS IN THREE DAYS—BY MIDNIGHT OF THE DAY AFTER TOMORROW.

DENIED
TWUP
KRASH
My the floor's just rotted through.
I SWEAR I'LL HIT YOU ONCE!!
JOOOOO

FINALLY ...

BAAAAM

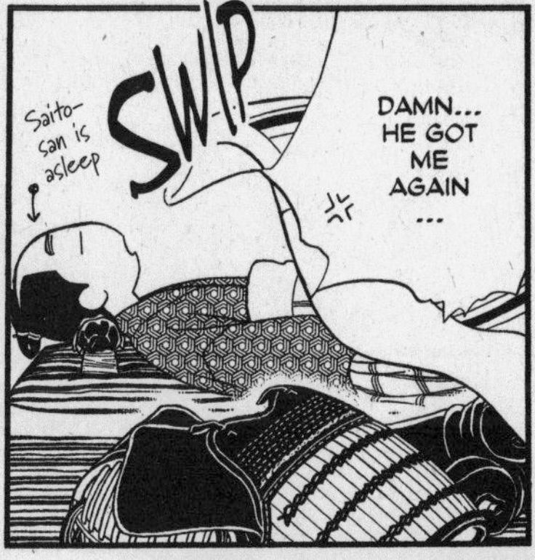

DAMN... HE GOT ME AGAIN ...
SWIP
Saito-san is asleep

WHAT THE HELL ARE YOU DOING HERE?
It's so hot.
JUST LET ME STAY HERE FOR ONE NIGHT, HIJIKATA-SAN.
I'll go somewhere else tomorrow.

OKITA SOJI IS NOT TO BE UNDER-ESTIMATED!!
And he uses some cheap tricks!!
He he.

WHAT SHOULD I DO...? IT'S BEEN TWO DAYS ALREADY...
IF I CAN'T GET A HIT BY TONIGHT ...
I'LL HAVE TO LEAVE.
Where are you Okita ...?
HA
WHY DO YOU LOOK SO HAPPY?
HE HE.
This is the Miyako flower.
MY WISH FINALLY COMES TRUE TONIGHT.
WHAT WOULD THAT BE?
IT'S A SECRET. ♡
IT MAKES OKITA-SENSEI SO HAPPY...
...TO THINK THAT I MIGHT LEAVE.

NO MATTER HOW HARD I TRY TO BECOME "BUSHI"...
Vice-captain Yamanami! The captain's calling you!
Okay.
HE NEVER INTENDED TO ACCEPT ME.
HE WANTED ME TO LEAVE FROM THE GET-GO...!!
HA
DAMN IT!

WUMP

KAMIYA-SAN!

ARE YOU ALL RIGHT?!

DON'T TOUCH ME!!

YOU JUST WANT ME TO LEAVE!
DON'T BE KIND TO ME!!
...BUT ...
IT SEEMS THAT YOU HAVE INJURED YOURSELF.
THERE'S BLOOD ON YOUR LEG.

I'M NOT INJURED...
!
!
NO...
MY HORSE HAS ARRIVED?!
"H-HORSE"?

I DON'T KNOW ...

BUT, WHEN I TURNED 14, MY FATHER TOLD ME THAT MY "HORSE" WOULD ARRIVE...

YOUR **FATHER** DID?!

HE HAD NO OTHER CHOICE BECAUSE MY MOTHER HAD ALREADY DIED! AND MY FATHER WAS A DOCTOR. DO YOU FIND IT STRANGE THAT HE COULD KNOW SO MUCH ABOUT WOMEN?

OH, THAT'S RIGHT.

RIGHT, AND WHAT DID YOUR FATHER SAY TO DO?

HE SAID, "DON'T PANIC BECAUSE IT'S NOT A DISEASE."

AND?!

"TELL FATHER IMMEDIATELY."
NOOOO, THAT DOESN'T HELP.

HIJIKATA-SAN! HIJIKATA-SAAAAN!
WHAT GOOD IS CALLING THE VICE-CAPTAIN?
Don't yell!!
USE THIS PAPER FOR NOW.
WE HAVE TO FIND SOME-ONE WHO KNOWS WHAT TO DO...
WHO WOULD KNOW ANYTHING IN THIS WOMAN-LESS HOUSE-HOLD?!
IT MUST BE A WOMAN ...
OH!
A WOMAN!
SHIMA-BARA!!!
AKESATO-SAN!!!!
SOJI?
WHERE ARE YOU GOING WITH KAMIYA?
WE'RE WORKING ON HIS HORSEMAN-SHIP!!

KAMIYA-SAN, HOLD ON TIGHTLY!
WE'RE ALMOST THERE!
DSH
DSH
DSH
DSH
IT'S OVER...
THIS IS HORRIBLE...
NOW'S THE WORST POSSIBLE TIME TO BECOME A WOMAN.
AKESATO-SAAAN!
...YOUR FIRST?!
Still getting ready for work.

WHAT SHOULD WE DO?
I HAVE TWO OLDER SISTERS, BUT I WAS KEPT IN THE DARK ON THESE MATTERS...
OF COURSE YOU WERE!
SLAM
I guess you're right...
OSEI-CHAN.
DON'T WORRY.

CHANGE INTO THIS UNDER-WEAR.
GIVE ME THE SOILED ONES.
I'M GOING TO TEACH YOU HOW TO MAKE A "HORSE."
MAKE A WHAT?

FIRST, FOLD THIS PAPER AND CONNECT TWO OF THEM...
YOU TIE THIS TO YOUR WAIST WITH A STRING.
IT LOOKS LIKE A HORSE'S SADDLE GIRTH, SO THAT'S WHY THEY CALL IT A "HORSE."

SHOCK
TH-TH-THIS THING IS SUP-POSED TO HOLD UP?!
IT WON'T SLIP OR LEAK...?!

OF COURSE IT DOES.
THAT'S WHY GIRLS HAVE TO STAY INSIDE AND STAY CALM FOR SEVEN DAYS OUT OF EACH MONTH.
SEVEN DAYS?!
OSEI-CHAN...!
YOU HAVE A SHITAOBI※ ON?!

WELL, OF COURSE...
I CAN'T BE WEARING A YUMOJI.※
.....

※ *Shitaobi* was another name for a loincloth. A *yumoji* was a woman's waistcloth.

OSEI-CHAN, PLEASE JUST QUIT.
YOU'VE GOTTEN YOUR REVENGE. WHY DO YOU HAVE TO GO TO SUCH LENGTHS TO STAY WITH THE MIBU-ROSHI?
AKESATO-SAN...
I FEEL SO SORRY FOR YOU. I DON'T KNOW WHAT TO DO...
A GIRL WITH SUCH A DELICATE BODY CARRY-ING TWO SWORDS...
YOU WANT TO GO THROUGH ALL THIS TO STAY CLOSE TO OKITA-SAN?
YES!!
...SUCH A QUICK RE-SPONSE.
This girl...

BUT IF THAT'S THE CAUSE, THEN WOULDN'T YOU RATHER QUIT AND BE HIS BRIDE?

BRIDE ?!

MAKE A HOME WITH OKITA-SAN, HAVE KIDS, AND RAISE THEM...

ISN'T THAT A GIRL'S TRUE HAPPINESS?

BUT THEN...

I WON'T BE ABLE TO PROTECT OKITA-SENSEI.

...

WHAT?
WHEN SENSEI IS FIGHTING, SOAKED IN BLOOD...
I DON'T WANT TO JUST STAY AT HOME AND PRAY.

EVEN IF I'M SCORNED FOR NOT BEING LADY-LIKE, MY BLISS IS TO PROTECT SENSEI.
FOR THAT, I'VE DECIDED THAT I'D EVEN BECOME AN *ONI* MYSELF!
OSEI-CHAN...
EVEN SO...
SNIFF
WHAT DID I DO TO DESERVE TO GET MY HORSE...?
I CAN'T TAKE SEVEN DAYS OFF EVERY MONTH! AND WITH THIS KIND OF TREATMENT, THERE'S NO WAY THEY WON'T KNOW WHAT'S GOING ON!
NOW I'LL BE THROWN OUT OF THE MIBU-ROSHI...
OSEI-CHAN...

WELL... SEEING YOUR DESPERATE FACE...
I REALLY CAN'T OBJECT, EVEN THOUGH I REALLY WANT YOU TO LEAVE.
...I'M SURE WE CAN FIGURE SOMETHING OUT...
WHAT?!
THERE'S A WAY?
BAM
AKESATO-SAN. ♡♡
IT'S NOTHING TO BOAST ABOUT, BUT...
WE HAVE TO TAKE CUSTOMERS HERE AFTER ONLY TWO DAYS' REST.

TWO DAYS! ONLY?!
SO WE USE SOMETHING CALLED AN "INSERT PAPER."
AND WE INSERT A PIECE OF *NOBEGAMI*.※

INSERT ...?!
IT'S STILL GOING TO BE DIFFICULT WITH YOUR DUTIES TO ONLY HAVE TWO DAYS...
YOU'RE GOING TO NEED AT LEAST THREE DAYS...

※A type of Japanese paper that was often used in the Kyoto area.

I CAN PULL OFF THREE DAYS!
IF I WORK ALL THE OTHER DAYS, THEN I THINK IT'LL WORK!!
REALLY?
THEN THERE MIGHT BE SOME-THING WE CAN DO.

I SAW YOUR *SHITAOBI* EARLIER AND THOUGHT...
IT WOULD BE MUCH MORE SECURE TO USE THE *SHITAOBI* THAN JUST TYING THE HORSE.
AND IF WE GET CREATIVE WITH WHAT WE LAY DOWN, LIKE AN OLD CLOTH, OR SOME OIL PAPER...
IT WOULD LAST MUCH LONGER THAN THE "HORSE" MADE OF PAPER!
THAT WOULD BE A MUCH BETTER "HORSE."

WE CAN ALSO GET CREATIVE WITH YOUR *SHITAOBI* ...
AND PUT A STRING ON IT LIKE A LOIN-CLOTH. IT MIGHT BE EASIER WHEN YOU HAVE TO GO TO THE BATHROOM.
It's the one that looks like this.
YOU'RE A GENIUS AKESATO-SAN!!
DON DON DON
HA!

THAT DRUM SOUND—WHAT TIME IS IT!?
HUH?
I THINK IT WAS ABOUT TEN?
TWO MORE HOURS AND IT'LL BE MIDNIGHT ...!?
IT'S NO USE...
EVEN IF I CAN DO SOMETHING ABOUT MY HORSE, WITH ONLY A LITTLE WHILE BEFORE MIDNIGHT...,
THERE'S NO WAY I CAN SUCCESSFULLY STRIKE OKITA-SENSEI!
WHAT'S WRONG OSEI-CHAN?
I'M SORRY, AKESATO-SAN.
YOU'VE DONE SO MUCH FOR ME BUT...

IN A HALF-HOUR'S TIME, IT'LL BE MIDNIGHT...
THE END OF MY CONTEST WITH KAMIYA-SAN... RIGHT...
OKITA-HAN?
AKESATO-SAN IS CALLING YOU.
Y-YES!

IS EVERYTHING ALL RIGHT WITH KAMIYA-SAN?
SHHH.
SHE JUST CALMED DOWN.

SHE SAID SHE'S FINALLY COME TO TERMS.
"COME TO TERMS"?

...OKITA-SENSEI ...
KAMI ...!?
WH-WHAT'S H-H-HAPPENED ...
THANK YOU FOR YOUR TROUBLES.
THROUGH THIS INCIDENT, I'VE REALIZED WHAT A BURDEN I AM TO YOU.
THERE WAS NO WAY FOR ME TO PERFECT MY SWORDSMANSHIP, NO MATTER HOW HARD I TRAIN...

I'M DEEPLY SORRY FOR BEING SUCH A BURDEN.
DON'T BE SILLY!
YOU HAVE IT ALL WRONG, KAMIYA-SAN!
IT WAS I WHO FEARED *YOU* BECAUSE YOU KEPT ON IMPROVING...
I SWORE I WOULDN'T DRAW MY SWORD...
AND YET, I SHOWED MY SWORD TO YOU...
...
BUT YOU ARE STILL A GIRL.
I KNEW THAT, EVENTUALLY, SUCH A DAY WOULD COME...
AND YOU WOULD HAVE TO LEAVE THE MIBU-ROSHI...
I JUST WANTED FOR YOU TO LEAVE, EVEN A DAY EARLY...
SO THAT YOU WOULD NOT BE HURT.
THAT WAS ALL I WISHED FOR.

YAY! SO THAT'S WHAT IT WAS!
OW!
BAP

...HUH?

GOTCHA.

MEN. ♡ OSEI-CHAN WINS!!
THANK YOU, AKESATO-SAN.
NOW I WON'T HAVE TO LEAVE THE MIBU-ROSHI. ♡
WOO-HOO!!
WHAT?!

IT'S MIDNIGHT! ♡
DON DON ♪
A SAMURAI NEVER GOES BACK ON HIS WORD! ♡
IT'S TOO LATE NOW! ♡
...

YOU BAM-BOOZLED MEEEEE!
BWA HA HA HA HA HA HA...
THAAAAT'S RIGHT!!!
OKITA SOJI, COMPLETELY DEFEATED.
ON A SIDE NOTE, IT BECAME QUITE CUSTOMARY FOR MENSTRUATING WOMEN TO USE A LOINCLOTH IN TIMES TO FOLLOW, BUT...
THAT IS YET ANOTHER DIGRES-SION.
HEY, WHAT HAPPENED TO KAMIYA-KUN?
HE SAID HE'S ON A "THREE DAY INDUL-GENCE."※

※Commonly used term in brothels, referring to staying over for multiple nights in a row.

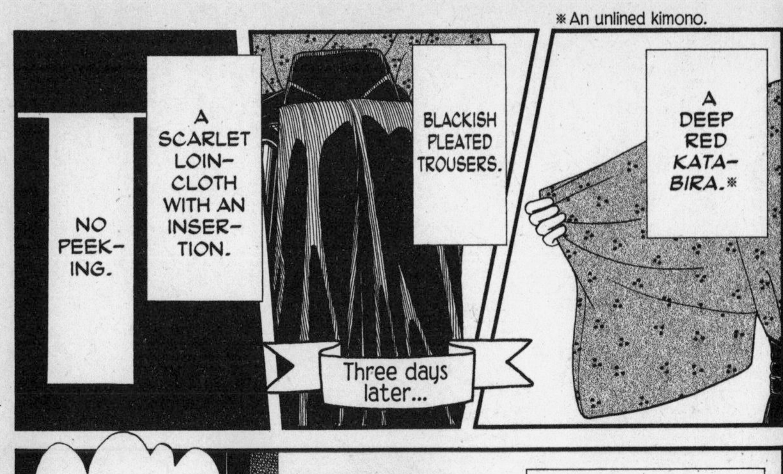

A DEEP RED KATA-BIRA.※
BLACKISH PLEATED TROUSERS.
Three days later...
A SCARLET LOIN-CLOTH WITH AN INSER-TION.
NO PEEK-ING.

※An unlined kimono.

ALL OF THESE ARE PART OF THE "ANTI-HORSE, WON'T STAND OUT IF SOMETHING HAPPENS" DRESS COLLECTION BY AKESATO-SAN.
THIS IS PERFECT!
NOW TO GO HOME!
KAMIYA SEIZABURO HAS JUST RETURNED!!

KYOTO "IROHA" KARUTA GAME

Wel-

わ

"WA"
WARAIKADO NI WA FUKU KITARU
"FORTUNE ENTERS AT THE MERRY DOOR"

KAMIYAAAA!
CAPTAIN SERIZAWA, W-W-WHAT IS IT?
WE HEARD! WE HEARD ABOUT THE BET WITH OKITA!!
HUH?
DON'T HOLD OUT ON US! ♡
HARADA-SAN?
YOU BET A "THREE DAY INDULGENCE" WITH SOJI—AND FOUGHT HIM—RIGHT?

AFTER ALL, YOUR LOVE FOR AKESATO GAVE YOU THE SKILL TO SCORE A HIT OFF OF SOJI. OH HOW AMAZING!
NAGA-KURA-SEN...
OOO... WHAT A GUY! WHAT A LOVER!
UH, UM, TODO-SEN...
DON'T BE SO NOISY, YOU DAMN IDIOTS!
DON'T YOU REMEMBER THAT TOSHI-SAN SAID IT WOULD BE A BAD EXAMPLE FOR THE OTHERS?
INOUE-SENSEI ...
NO NEED TO WORRY KAMIYA, I'VE TOLD THAT STICK-IN-THE-MUD HIJIKATA THAT YOU HAVE "OFFICIAL BUSINESS" TO DO THREE DAYS A MONTH. ♡
THAT'S RIGHT, SO ALL WE HAVE TO DO IS NOT TELL THE OTHERS. ♡
WE'RE NOT THE KIND OF PEOPLE WHO WOULD SAY, "THAT'S NOT FAIR."
R... RIGHT... THANK YOU VERY MUCH?
SO ... YOU KNOW?
JUST US IS FINE.
REGALE US WITH YOUR THREE-DAY HEROIC EPISODE.

"HEROIC EPISODE"...?
GOD!
YOU'RE GOING TO PRETEND THAT NOTHING HAPPENED.
SO, HOW MANY TIMES DID YOU "KILL" AKESATO IN THREE DAYS?
BWOOSH
HOW MANY...?
AND HE BLUSHES...
HOO-BOY
IT'S JUST TOO CUTE...
TH-THESE PEOPLE...
QUIT IT GUYS.
VICE-CAPTAIN YAMANAMI...
Even Serizawa-sensei
IT'S NOT SOMETHING TO TEASE HIM ABOUT.
KAMIYA-KUN'S NOT PLAYING.
I'M SURE HE'S FOUND TRUE LOVE.

LOVE ...!!
DON'T BE PRE-SUMPTUOUS, YAMANAMI-SAN.
WHETHER IT'S LOVE OR PLAY, IT'S ALL THE SAME IN BED!!
GAHAHA HAHAH
YOU'RE JUST SO SERIOUS!
THOSE FILTHY ANIMALS!!

WHY OH WHY DID I EVER MISS THESE GUYS?!

in Osaka

VULGAR! DIRTY-MINDED! THE ENEMIES OF WOMEN!!

Hup

TMP

HEY, WHERE DID KAMIYA GO?

AND, ON TOP OF EVERYTHING...

THESE GUYS THINK I'M A LECH ...?!

That means ...

SHOCK

I'M THE "ROUGHNECK SHOGUN OF BUNKYU" ...?!

No one's said anything *that* exaggerated (heh)

OKITA-SENSEI!!!!!
WHY COULDN'T HE THINK OF A MORE DECENT EXCUSE...?!
OKITA-SENSEI WAS WITH SAITO-SENSEI IN THE ANNEX YARD.
THANKS.
OF ALL THINGS, AN "INDULGENCE."
I CAN ONLY IMAGINE THAT THIS IS HIS REVENGE...
FOR ME AND AKESATO-SAN TRICKING HIM.
OKI ...!
HUH?

SENSEI SEEMS DIFFERENT FROM USUAL.
BOTH OF THEM ARE HOLDING *REAL SWORDS!*
P-PLEASE STOP, OKITA-SENSEI!!

YOU TOO, SAITO-SENSEI!
WHAT'S HAPPENED THAT THE TWO OF YOU ARE FIGHTING WITH REAL SWORDS?!
KAMIYA.
DRAW YOUR SWORD, KAMIYA-SAN!
THIS WORKS OUT WELL.
IF I CAN'T FIGHT SAITO-SAN, THEN YOU CAN OCCUPY MY TIME.
I-I DON'T WANT TO!
I CAN'T DRAW MY SWORD AGAINST YOU.
WHY?
I...
CAN KILL YOU.

BLOOD–
THIRSTY.

THUMP
...
HA
HA
HA
...GOOD FOR YOU FOR TAKING THE BLOW.
BUT IF YOU STOP A KATANA FRONT-FACE LIKE YOU JUST DID, IT WILL SURELY BREAK.
YOU MUST FENCE OFF "STRENGTH" IN ORDER TO KILL IT.
HOW-EVER...
EVEN NOW, IF I HAD NOT STOPPED MY HAND, YOUR HEAD WOULD HAVE SPLIT, JUST AS YOUR KATANA.

YOU MIGHT HAVE GOTTEN AWAY WITH A DENT IN YOUR HEAD WITH THIS DULLED KATANA.
DULLED ...?
BY THE WAY, WHY ARE YOU SITTING DOWN SO LEISURELY?
I HAVEN'T PUT AWAY MY KATANA YET.
B-BECAUSE ... MY BROTHER'S *DAITO* ...!
WHEN YOU'VE LOST YOUR *DAITO*, THEN DRAW YOUR *SHOTO*.
IF YOU LOSE YOUR *SHOTO*, THEN USE YOUR SHEATH.
IF YOU LOSE YOUR SHEATH, THEN FIGHT WITH YOUR BARE HANDS.
NO ONE WILL WAIT FOR YOU IN THE MIDDLE OF A BATTLE!
Y-YES!

OH.
KAMIYA!
slightly anemic
HEY, OKITA-SAN.
...
KAMIYA DOESN'T LOOK WELL.
DON'T YOU THINK HE SHOULD REST A LITTLE?
PROBABLY EXHAUSTED FROM PLAYING AROUND.
NOTHING WORTHY OF SYMPATHY.
I WONDER WHAT IT IS...
OKITA-SENSEI ISN'T THE SAME.
I'VE GOTTEN USED TO HIS HARSH WORDS, BUT...
I FEEL LIKE I'VE NEVER HEARD...
...SUCH A COLD VOICE FROM HIM.
I GUESS WE HAVE NO CHOICE. FOR SAITO-SAN'S SAKE...
YOU MAY REST UNTIL IT'S TIME FOR PATROL—ONE HOUR FROM NOW.

HE WON'T EVEN LOOK BACK.
WHAT IS THIS?
OKITA-SENSEI.
TRUE BLOOD-THIRST...
IS THIS WHAT IT'S LIKE TO BE HATED?
BUT WHY...
HUP
HUH?
YOU'RE SO LIGHT.
S-SAITO-SENSEI.

I SEE.
REMNANTS OF YOUR "THREE-DAY INDULGENCE," HUH?
WELL, SOMEBODY JUST SCORED A POINT OFF OF ME. BANG.
PLEASE DON'T SAY THINGS LIKE THAT SO CALMLY.

AND YOU SMELL GOOD.
UM, THAT WAS BECAUSE AKESATO-SAN SOAKED MY CLOTHES WITH INCENSE.
It's odor-protection for your horse.
the shade of a tree.
I'll get down now. I'm fine.

OH.
I'm dizzy from exhaustion.
...

SORRY.
FWUP

OH, FORGIVE ME.
I JUST THOUGHT FOR A SECOND THAT...

...YOU WERE A GIRL.

ULP

WHAT DO YOU THINK YOU'RE DOING?!
TH-THIS MAN...!!

FORGIVE MY PREVIOUS MISAPPRE-HENSION.
BUT REALLY...
YOU'VE GOT QUITE AN IMPRESSIVE PACKAGE.

WH-WHAT MADE YOU THINK THAT I WAS A GIRL?
I'M SO GLAD THAT I STUFFED MY *SHITAOBI* WITH A LOT OF THINGS.

THERE ARE NO EXACT REASONS BEHIND MY HUNCHES.
BUT, MOST OF THE TIME, THE REASONS FOLLOW.

I'M RARELY WRONG, BUT...
I GUESS YOU WERE WRONG THIS TIME. *HA HA HA.*

YOU CAN TRUST OKITA-SAN.
HUH?

NOW WHAT ARE YOU SAYING?
I TOLD YOU, THERE ARE NO EXACT REASONS BEHIND MY HUNCHES.

BUT MY HUNCHES HAVE NOT BEEN WRONG— SO FAR.

...

...WHEN I CLOSE MY EYES, IT'S ANI-UE'S VOICE.

YOU'RE TELLING ME...
...TO HANG IN THERE, RIGHT?
SAITO-SENSEI.

IT'S ALL IN MY MIND THAT HE HATES ME.

I SHOULD JUST TRUST OKITA-SENSEI.

KAMI-YA?

WHAT HAPPENED TO YOUR *DAITO*?

I UNWITTINGLY LOST IT. IT SPLIT IN HALF.

MORON!

I'LL LEND YOU MY SPARE.

OKITA-SENSEI'S BEEN RAGING THESE PAST THREE DAYS.

I DON'T KNOW HOW MAD HE'D GET IF HE FOUND OUT ABOUT YOUR ILL-PREPAREDNESS.

"THESE PAST THREE DAYS"?
I WONDER WHY...
HE'S FOUGHT WITH SAITO-SENSEI WITH DULLED KATANA—LOOKING REALLY FEROCIOUS...
Those two could actually kill each other, even with a dulled katana!
IT'S LIKE...

YOU JUST WANT TO ASK HIM, "WHAT DO YOU HATE SO MUCH?"
...
HEY, KAMIYA...

HERE'S MY *DAITO* ...
THERE'S NO NEED FOR THAT.
O-OKITA-SENSEI!
A *WAKIZASHI* IS PLENTY FOR KAMIYA-SAN.
!
B-BUT...
KAMIYA HAS A TIMING DISADVANTAGE BECAUSE OF HIS SHORT ARMS...
HE JUST NEEDS TO MOVE TO COMPENSATE FOR DISTANCE.
A *DAITO* WILL ONLY BURDEN HIM.
...ARE YOU SAYING ...
THAT I AM NOT WORTHY OF CARRYING MY BROTHER'S *DAITO*?!

WELL ...
UNFORTUNATELY, YES.

That was harsh.
Does that mean that Kamiya doesn't deserve to carry a daito?
He's not bushi if he's only carrying one sword.

IF THERE'RE NO OTHER QUESTIONS, THEN WE'LL GET GOING.

...YOU REALLY DON'T WANT TO ACCEPT IT, HUH?

ARE YOU REALLY THAT MAD...

...THAT I WON THE BET?!

THAT IS NOT SOMETHING WE NEED DISCUSS NOW!

A COLD VOICE FILLED WITH HATE...

OKITA-SENSEI WAS MAD...
...THAT I SCORED A POINT FROM HIM IN SUCH A DEVIOUS MANNER.

OF COURSE, I THOUGHT THAT IT MIGHT BE CHEATING A LITTLE, BUT...
I DIDN'T DOUBT THAT SENSEI WOULD LAUGH ABOUT IT AND FORGIVE ME.

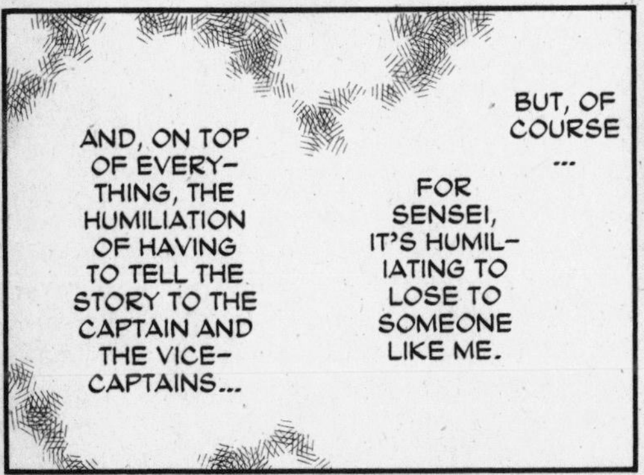
BUT, OF COURSE...
FOR SENSEI, IT'S HUMILIATING TO LOSE TO SOMEONE LIKE ME.
AND, ON TOP OF EVERYTHING, THE HUMILIATION OF HAVING TO TELL THE STORY TO THE CAPTAIN AND THE VICE-CAPTAINS...

WHAT SHOULD I DO? OF COURSE HE HATES ME.
I MADE A GREAT SWORDSMAN INTO A LAUGHING-STOCK.

...OOPS?
ALL ALONE

I'VE LOST THEM!
WHAT SHOULD I DO? DAMN IT, I WAS SO DEEP IN THOUGHT...
WHAT'S THE ROUTE TODAY?
...WE WOULD APPRECIATE IT IF YOU COULD TELL US THE DETAILS OF THAT!
!!

NOT BAD.
THE MIBU WOLVES ALWAYS TRAVEL IN PACKS, BUT...
AND HE'S SUCH A YOUNGLING.
WE'LL GET GREAT INFORMATION IF WE JUST *PLAY* WITH HIM A LITTLE.
THEY'RE ANTI-BAKUFU?!
I CAN'T BELIEVE I ONLY HAVE MY *WAKIZASHI*.
MMMM!
DAMN IT, AT LEAST I'LL DIE GRACEFULLY!!
DON'T MOVE!
MOVE AND I GUARANTEE YOU'LL BE IN SERIOUS PAIN!!
MMMM!
MMMM!
MMMM!
BAP
SLUMP
WHA—?!
WHAT HAPPENED!?
DID HE DIE?

...WHAT THE HELL DO YOU THINK!!
WHAT?!
DSH
THIS LITTLE WHELP!
IT'S SO EASY TO DRAW! WHY? HOW COME?
IT'S SO EASY TO MOVE!
IT'S BECAUSE MY KATANA'S SHORTER!

"HE JUST NEEDS TO MOVE TO COMPEN-SATE FOR DISTANCE."
OKITA-SENSEI.
IS THIS WHAT YOU MEANT?!
ANI-UE'S *DAITO* WAS TOO LONG AND HEAVY FOR ME.
BUT, EVEN THEN ...
I CAN'T BELIEVE ...
... THESE GUYS.
HOW SLOW THEY ARE COMPARED TO OKITA-SENSEI.

KAMIYA-
SAN!!

...
...
...ARE YOU WOUNDED?
OKITA-SENSEI ... ... YOU'RE LIKE THE WIND ...
ANSWER MY QUESTION!!
NO, I'M FINE!!

I'M SO GLAD ...!!
BONK
OKITA-SENSEI ...?
IT'S ALL MY FAULT THAT YOU ENDED UP STAYING.
IF YOU HAD DIED JUST NOW ...
I JUST DON'T KNOW WHAT I'D DO...
sigh
YOUR FAULT ...?
I STAYED OF MY OWN FREE WILL...
YOU'RE WRONG.
IT'S MY RESPONSIBILITY FOR ACCEPTING YOUR CHALLENGE.

YOU COULD HAVE JUST LED A PEACEFUL GIRL'S LIFE, BUT—
MY CONCEITED-NESS IN THINKING THAT I WOULD NEVER LOSE THE BET HAS RUINED YOUR FATE.
WHEN I THOUGHT OF THAT, I CURSED MY THOUGHT-LESSNESS.
THESE PAST THREE DAYS ...
MY ONLY THOUGHTS WERE OF WISHING THAT SOMEONE WOULD PUNISH ME.
BUT THAT'S NOT POSSI-BLE.
YOU ARE SO STRONG.
SAITO-SAN HAS SUCH A GOOD HUNCH.
HE CAN TELL, NO MATTER HOW BLOOD-THIRSTY I TRY TO BE...
THAT I'M NOT REALLY CHARG-ING...
YOU WERE THE OBJECT OF YOUR OWN HATRED!

POW
STOP MESSING AROUND ...!!
KA...
KAMIYA-SAN...?
A SAMURAI NEVER GOES BACK ON HIS WORD!!
WHATEVER YOUR FEEL-INGS, AS LONG AS YOU LOST THE BET, YOU SHOULD KEEP YOUR PROMISE OF ACCEPTING ME AS A MAN!!

OF COURSE!
THAT'S WHY I MADE YOUR MONTHLY, THREE-DAY VACATION AS MANLY A REASON AS POSSIBLE!
THAT WAS NOT NECESSARY!!
I'M ALSO THINKING ABOUT HOLDING PRACTICE SESSIONS THAT WILL BETTER SUIT YOUR NEEDS...
THEN...
IF YOU REALLY ARE GOING TO ACCEPT ME AS A MAN...
THEN WHY DO YOU TRY TO BEAR THE RESPONSI-BILITY...
...THAT ANOTHER MAN *CHOSE* FOR HIMSELF?!
...
UH...

BUT YOU'RE STILL A CHILD...
STOP JERK-ING ME AROUND!!
SLAM
Who do you think the roughneck shogun of Bukyu is?!
BASH
BASH
OW!
OW!
AHH, I GIVE UP, I GIVE UP!
I GIVE UP!
Kamiyaaaa!
Are you there?
Okita-sensei!
Where did you get that bruise?
THUS THE DAY THAT KAMIYA SEIZABURO WOULD BE ACCEPTED AS A TRUE MAN BY OKITA SOJI CAME TO PASS.
HMPH.

AND THE NEXT DAY...
I WAS HOPING THAT IT WOULD HAVE COME IN TIME FOR YESTERDAY'S PATROL, BUT...
A NEW *DAITO*?!
I WENT TO GO LOOK FOR ONE THE DAY YOU DECIDED TO STAY, BUT THE *KOSHIRAE*※ TOOK SOME TIME.
IT'S ABOUT FOUR MEASURES LONGER THAN YOUR *WAKIZASHI*, BUT THERE'S A *HI*✻ IN IT, SO...
IT'S LIGHT! SO MUCH LIGHTER THAN ANI-UE'S!!
THANK YOU SO MUCH, OKITA-SENSEI!!
BUT...

✻A rut in the katana that allows it to be lighter without compromising its strength.

※A decoration put in the hilt and the sheath.

※A *kogai* was used as a comb and a decorative hairpiece.

WHY DID YOU HAVE IT MADE WITH A *KOGAI*※ THAT HAS NO USE IN BATTLE?
it's attached here
WELL...
BECAUSE ?!
You're a girl... I... Couldn't help myself...?
I THOUGHT SO!
WHY?!
Um...
QUIT JERKING ME AROUND!
BAAAAM
BSH BSH
BSH BSH
I GIVE UP!
I GIVE UP! KAMIYA-SAN IS A MAN AMONG MEN!
OWWWW!
Don't die Soji.
HEY, THERE'S SOME WATER-MELON...
It's good.

"KA"
か
KAERU NO TSURA NI MIZU "LIKE WATER OFF A DUCK'S BACK"
I'm all right.
KYOTO "IROHA" KARUTA GAME

SSSSS

JULY OF THE THIRD YEAR OF BUNKYU (AUGUST OF 1863).

MIBU-ROSHI RESIDENCE—THE SHOJI HOUSE.

GAAAWD, I CAN'T STAND IT!

CAN'T IT JUST STOP RAINING ALREADY?!

our heroine

KYOTO "IROHA" KARUTA GAME

よ

"YO"
YOMETOME KASA NO UCHI
"FAR FOWLS HAVE FAIR FEATHERS"

KAMIYA'S IN A BAD MOOD.
AREN'T WE ALL IN THE SAME BOAT?
IT'S BEEN RAINING NON-STOP FOR THREE DAYS.
It's hot too!
STUCK PRACTICING INDOORS WHERE THERE'S NO ROOM TO SWING OUR *SHINAI* AROUND—EVEN A MATURE MAN LIKE MYSELF IS IN A BAD MOOD.
A ROTTEN ENDING IS INDEED LETHAL.
Only practice tsuki, tsuki, tsuki, tsuki, tsuki.
That's all we do.
GOD, I WANT A DOJO.
WHAT?
YOU WANT A DOJO, KAMIYA?

AHHHH!
C-C-CAPTAIN SERIZAWA!
YOU SHOULD BUILD ONE.
ISN'T THE PROPERTY IN FRONT OF THE YAGI HOUSE JUST SITTING THERE?
IT'S NOT THAT SIMPLE.
IT'LL COST MONEY FOR BOTH THE MATERIALS AND THE MANPOWER— AND WE HAVE A VERY TIGHT BUDGET.
DON'T BE AN IMBECILE!!
WE SERVE THE COUNTRY!
THERE'RE PLENTY OF PEOPLE WHO WOULD LOVE TO GIVE US MONEY!
LEAVE IT TO ME!!
P- PLEASE WAIT, SERIZAWA-SENSEI.
HE'S TRYING TO EXTORT MONEY FROM THE MERCHANTS AGAIN?!
WHAT IS IT, KAMIYA?

WELL... UM...
OH, I JUST WANTED TO REMIND YOU THAT YOU HAVE ANOTHER NEW SET OF CLOTHES ON...
OH, THAT'S RIGHT. I CAME HERE BECAUSE I WANTED YOU TO SEE IT!
IT REALLY LOOKS GREAT ON YOU!
YOU'RE SUCH A FLATTERER, OKITA! ♡♡
I WOULDN'T MIND HEARING MORE! ♡
came around to the entrance
SERIZAWA-SENSEI!!!
WHAT?
THE BILL COLLECTOR FROM HISHIYA CAME, AND—
AND WHAT...? I'VE TOLD YOU TO IRON THINGS OUT AND HOLD HIM OFF!

THE THING IS, INSTEAD OF THE HEAD CLERK, HE SENT THE MISSUS.

SHE'S INSISTING THAT SHE WON'T LEAVE UNLESS SHE SEES YOU...

WHAT OF THE MISSUS?!

YELL AT HER LIKE THE CLERK AND GIVE HER A PIECE OF YOUR MIND!

YES, BUT IT'S JUST THAT ...

I can't believe that's what they've been doing.

※ As opposed to silk textiles, which are referred to as "*gofuku*," "*futomono*" refers to cotton and linen textiles.

YOU CAN'T TAKE A LITTLE JOKE, KAMIYA-SAN.
HISHIYA IS THE LARGE *FUTOMONO*※ WHOLESALER ON THE SHIJO-HORIKAWA!
FROM THE SOUND OF IT, THEY'VE BEEN REFUSING TO PAY THEIR DEBT...
AND SERIZAWA-SENSEI'S BAD REPUTATION PRECEDES HIM—ESPECIALLY HIS VIOLENT BEHAVIOR AT THE TEAHOUSES AND TOWARD MONEY-LENDERS!
IF WE DON'T DO SOMETHING ABOUT IT, EVEN THE PRESTIGE OF OUR PARTY...!!
EVERYBODY'S GONE
WHAT "LITTLE JOKE"?!
THE YAGI HOUSEHOLD

OH, YAGI-SAN.
WHERE IS MY GUEST?
SERIZAWA-SENSEI?
I'M SO GRATEFUL.
YOU'VE COME BACK!
!
B-BMP

I'M HISHIYA TAHEI'S WIFE, UME.
IT IS AN HONOR TO MEET YOU.
AH
UM...
WELL...
M-MY NAME IS SERIZAWA KAMO!
I'M SORRY TO BOTHER YOU RIGHT NOW, BUT AS FOR THE BILL FOR YOUR CLOTHES...
R-RIGHT, AND HOW MUCH WOULD THAT BE?
YES, IT'S ABOUT 30 *RYO*...
I-I SEE.
WE'LL PAY... THAT IS, WE'D LIKE TO PAY, BUT WE'RE SLIGHTLY ILL-PREPARED AT THE MOMENT.
I UNDERSTAND...
THEN I'LL COME BACK TOMORROW...
I-I'M TERRIBLY ASHAMED. BY TOMORROW...
I'M SURE WE'LL HAVE THE MONEY BY TOMORROW, OUME-DONO.

NO.
I'M THE ONE ASKING FOR YOUR PATIENCE.
I THOUGHT YOU WOULD BE A HARD-HEARTED PERSON.
LOVE
FOR YOU TO HAVE TURNED OUT TO BE SUCH A KIND MAN ...
IS SUCH A PLEASANT SURPRISE.
WELL, I'LL BE ON MY WAY NOW.
R-RIGHT.
SORRY FOR YOUR TROUBLES.
SAKICHI, LET'S GO.
hmmm
YES, OUME-SAN.
GLARE

...
SO, WHAT DID YOU THINK, SENSEI?!
THAT SEX APPEAL DESPITE BEING THE WIFE OF A HARD-ASS MERCHANT.
DID YOU SEE HER FACE WHEN SHE SAID "A KIND PERSON♡"?!
I THINK PERCHANCE SHE FANCIES YOU.
DON'T BE CRUDE—SHE'S SOMEONE ELSE'S WIFE!
THAT'S THE BEST PART! ♡
AN ILLICIT LOVE AFFAIR!
NO, THAT'S WRONG!!
IT GOES AGAINST MY PRINCIPLES AS A BUSHI TO STEAL SOMEONE'S WIFE!
Everyone is thinking, "I didn't know you had principles," but all choose to keep their mouths shut.
...

BUT WHO CAN STOP THE FLAMES OF LOVE, ONCE THEY'VE BEEN LIT?
OH, OUME.
All think, "the flames of love?" But, again, no one dares say anything.
...THIS ISN'T GOOD.
YES!
YOU'RE ABSOLUTELY RIGHT!
WOW, KAMIYA-SAN!
YOU'RE SOAKED.
YOU CAN STILL CATCH A COLD, EVEN IN THE SUMMER.
I'M SORRY.
LET'S GO HOME.
...DO MEN...
...ALL LIKE WOMEN LIKE *THAT*?

HUH?
I SAW HER GO BY.
I AGREE, SHE'S A BEAUTIFUL WOMAN, BUT...
REALLY?
I WAS MORE TAKEN BY HER MAGNIFICENT BREASTS THAN HER FACE.
DWAH?
ACK
YOU ARE SO PERVERTED!!
HA HA HA HA!
I'M STILL NO MATCH FOR THE "ROUGH-NECK SHOGUN OF BUNKYU"!
he he!
...I WONDER IF OKITA-SENSEI ALSO...
Feels good!
...LIKES THAT KIND OF FEMININE WOMAN...

...THERE'S NO TIME TO BE THINKING ABOUT SUCH THINGS, SEIZABURO!
SERIZAWA-SENSEI'S SITUATION IS THE URGENT MATTER AT HAND.
RIGHT!
IF LEFT ALONE, HE'LL PROBABLY GO TO TOWN TO EXTORT MONEY.
I DON'T HAVE MUCH TIME TO THINK.
THUS...
I CAME HERE, WELL AWARE OF MY RUDE-NESS.
TO ASK CAPTAIN KONDO TO HAVE A WORD WITH CAPTAIN SERIZAWA AS SOON AS POSSIBLE!
I BEG YOU TO HEAR ME OUT.
HUMMM...
...SOJI!!

HUH?
WHERE'S SOJI?
SOMEONE GO GET HIM!!
YES SIR!
TMP TMP TMP

TMP TMP
UM... VICE-CAPTAIN HIJI-KATA?
You're not going to hit him again are you...?

YOU CALLED, HIJIKATA-SAN?
FLASH
just took a bath
Oh, Kamiya-san. Hey.
PUT SOME DAMN CLOTHES ON!!

YOU RUSHED ME.
OH, WHO CARES.
JUST TAKE THIS CHILD AWAY!
oh god

WHAT?!
HEY, TOSHI...
DON'T LET THE LIKES OF KAMIYA COME OUT AND BE SO ASSERTIVE!
You don't have to put it like that.
!!
GRRRR
I APOLOGIZE.
THAT POOR EXCUSE FOR A VICE-CAPTAIN ...!
CALM DOWN.
AAARGH
WHAT DID YOU DO?
I HAVEN'T DONE ANYTHING WRONG!
I JUST ASKED KONDO-SENSEI TO HAVE A WORD WITH SERIZAWA-SENSEI...
OH.
WELL, OF COURSE HIJIKATA-SAN'S GOING TO KICK YOU OUT.

WHY?!
THERE'S A REASON WHY KONDO-SENSEI CAN'T GIVE HIS OPINION TO SERIZAWA-SENSEI.
AND KONDO-SENSEI'S NOT THE KIND OF PERSON WHO WOULD GIVE EXCUSES FOR THAT—A FACT THE *ONI* VICE-CAPTAIN IS WELL AWARE OF.
...GAH?
SERIZAWA-SENSEI IS ACTUALLY THE MIBU-ROSHI'S GREAT BENEFACTOR.
HUH?!
YOU MAY NOT KNOW THIS, BUT...
THE MIBU-ROSHI WAS ORIGINALLY A VOLUNTEER TROOP CREATED IN EDO BY THE BAKUFU, TO PROTECT THE SHOGUN WHEN HE WENT TO KYOTO.
天然理心流
試衛館道場
TO KYOTO?
YEAH!
KUBO-SAMA※ IS FINALLY GOING TO GET SERIOUS ABOUT EXCLUSIONISM AND HE'S GOING TO KYOTO TO COOPERATE WITH THE EMPEROR!
AS MEN, THERE'S NO WAY WE'RE NOT GOING TO BE A PART OF THIS, ISAMI-SAN!
LET'S GO!!

Sign: Ten'nen Rishin-ryu Shieikan-dojo

※Refers to the shogun. At the time, anti-foreign sentiment (*joi*) was quite common among the Japanese.

HOWEVER, KIYO-KAWA HACHIRO, WHO SUGGESTED THE CREATION OF A TROOP, WAS UNDER THE PRE-TENSE THAT HE WAS A PRO-BAKUFU EXCLUSIONIST. HE WAS ACTUALLY A SHINSEI-JOI-HA.※
AND, AS SOON AS THEY GOT TO KYOTO, HE LECTURED OVER 200 ROSHI AND TRIED TO CONVERT THEM TO THE WAYS OF SONNO-HA.

SO THAT'S WHEN THE SHIEIKAN, LED BY KONDO-SENSEI, AND...

WE WILL NEVER TURN OUR BACK TO THE EMPEROR, BUT SINCE WE'VE ANSWERED THE BAKUFU'S CALL AND HAVE COME TO KYOTO, CHANGING SIDES WILL GO AGAINST OUR BUSHIDO!!

I'VE NEVER EVEN HEARD OF TEN'NEN RISHIN-RYU, BUT...
KONDO-UJI'S BUSHIDO MAKES SENSE.

THE FIVE EX-TENGU PARTY LED BY SERIZAWA-SENSEI STOOD UP.
I FEEL THE SAME WAY!!

EVEN I WAS ONCE A MEMBER OF THE MITO TENGU, AND MY LOYALTY TO THE EMPEROR WILL NEVER WITHER, BUT...
I CANNOT AGREE WITH YOUR WAYS!!

※Those from the Mito Clan who were for the reformation of the clan system. Anti-foreign sentiment and supporting the emperor were some of their fundamental characteristics.

AFTER A BITTER DISAGREEMENT, MANY OF THE ROSHI WENT BACK TO EDO WITH KIYOKAWA...
AND THE 13 OF US WHO DECIDED TO CARRY OUT OUR ORIGINAL INTENTIONS WENT TO ASK FOR THE GUARDIANSHIP OF THE PROTECTOR OF KYOTO, LORD MATSUDAIRA KATAMORI.
HOWEVER, AS UNACCOMPLISHED COUNTRY BUSHI, WE WEREN'T EVEN ALLOWED TO SUBMIT A PETITION.
Katamori is very busy.
Come back another time!
THAT WAS WHEN—
MEN, DO NOT BE WARY!
MY BROTHER IS AT THE MITO FAMILY'S※ MANSION IN KYOTO.
EVEN IF IT MEANS I HAVE TO BEG, I'LL HAVE KATAMORI SEE US!
SO, THANKS TO SERIZAWA-SENSEI'S HEROIC EFFORTS...
OUR PETITION WAS HEARD BY THE PROTECTOR, AND...
THE MIBU-ROSHI WAS BORN.

※The Mito Tokugawa family, one of the three branch families of the house of Tokugawa.

I HAD NO IDEA ...
KONDO-SENSEI AND COMPANY ALL KNOW...
WHERE SERIZAWA-SENSEI HAS BORROWED HIS MONEY FROM, AND HOW HE IS SPENDING IT.
THEY'VE EVEN TAKEN CARE OF SOME OF IT IN CONFI-DENCE.
WHAT?!
BUT THEY PROBABLY DON'T SAY ANYTHING TO HIS FACE BECAUSE—
HE WAS THE GREAT BENE-FACTOR OF THE MIBU-ROSHI.
THEY WANT TO BELIEVE ...
...IN SERIZAWA-SENSEI'S SENSE OF BUSHIDO...
...THAT AGREED WITH KONDO-SENSEI'S BACK THEN.
...!

EVEN I UNDER-STAND—

THAT SERIZAWA-SENSEI'S NOT ***ALL*** EVIL...

AT FIRST I WAS SHOCKED ...
I'VE EVEN LOOKED DOWN AT HIM FOR BEING SUCH A VIOLENT DRUNK, BUT ...
NOW I'VE SEEN A DIFFERENT SIDE OF HIM.
THAT'S EVEN MORE REASON FOR DOING SOMETHING ABOUT HIS POOR REPUTATION IN TOWN...
Let's go.
It is a custom of Kyoto to dress casually too!
ARE YOU GOING TO GO DRINK, SERIZAWA-SENSEI!?
WILL YOU TAKE ME TOO!? ♡
DSH
GOD, THAT PERSON IS ALWAYS...
ALWAYS ...!
...SERIZAWA-SENSEI!

WILL YOU TAKE ME AS WELL?!
IS HE ...?!
OH, KAMIYA. HOW RARE FOR YOU TO ASK! ♡
OF COURSE! ♡
...
at a loss for words
SMIRK
I KNEW IT.
BWA HA HA HA
WHAT?
you shouldn't laugh like that
I GET IT NOW—
OKITA-SENSEI WAS ALWAYS TAKING CARE OF THINGS!

EVEN I HAVE COME TO UNDER-STAND THAT, OKITA-SENSEI.
THE FIRST ORDER OF DUTY IS TO GO GET FUNDS!
YOU COULD AT LEAST SAY "YOU'VE GROWN."
SERIZAWA-SENSEI, LET ME TREAT YOU TODAY!
YOU WILL!
♪
YES!
I KNOW THE PERFECT PLACE TO COOL DOWN. ESPECIALLY ON A NIGHT AS HOT AS TONIGHT.
IS THIS THE PLACE YOU WERE TALKING ABOUT?

SURE IS.
IT'S CALLED THE "KAMO'S RIVERSIDE," SO I THOUGHT IT WOULD BE PERFECT FOR YOU. ♡
And much cheaper than a teahouse. ♡
BUT WHO IS GOING TO POUR OUR DRINKS?
AM I NOT GOOD ENOUGH, SERIZAWA-SENSEI?
KAMIYA-SAN?!
PLIP
WILL GOOD SAKE BE RUINED IF A MAN POURS IT...?
WHAT ARE YOU SAYING? MY DEAR KAMIYA...
THERE'S NOTHING WRONG WITH THE SAKE YOU'VE POURED!
OH, GOOD.
THEN PLEASE HAVE ANOTHER ONE. ♡
I knew recently...
she's getting clever, but...
IT'S DELICIOUS!!
TASTES FANTASTIC, KAMIYA!!

MAY I HAVE A WORD WITH YOU, KAMIYA-SAN!
just a moment
YES?
WHY DID YOU COME HERE?
BECAUSE I WANTED TO HELP YOU?
YOU NEEDN'T WORRY ABOUT SUCH THINGS! NOW GO HOME!
"SUCH THINGS"!
EVEN I'M CONCERNED ABOUT SERIZAWA-SENSEI'S VIOLENT BEHAVIOR!
...IF YOU DON'T LISTEN TO ME ...!
GLOMP
!!

UM...
OKITA-SEN...
B-BMP B-BMP
SHH!
OUME-SAN IS HERE!
!
WHY SHOULD WE HIDE JUST BECAUSE THAT BIG-CHESTED HARLOT IS HERE?
KAMIYA-SAN, BE QUIET!
...THAT COUNTRY SAMURAI WAS TOO EASY.
HE SAID THAT HE'D PAY TOMORROW.
REALLY? YOU'RE REALLY SOME-THING.
I SURE PICKED THE RIGHT WOMAN TO FALL FOR.

YOU'RE JUST ALL TALK.
WHY DON'T YOU MAKE ME YOUR REAL WIFE THEN?
I TOLD YOU...
I MARRIED INTO MY WIFE'S FAMILY!
?!
YOU'RE DETEST-ABLE.
YOU SAY THAT, BUT YOU LOVE HER.
EVERY-BODY SAYS YOU'RE A COUPLE OF LOVE-BIRDS!
DON'T BE STUPID.
I TOLD YOU TIME AND TIME AGAIN, YOU'RE THE ONLY ONE...
LET'S GO, KAMIYA-SAN
This is an adults-only con-versation.
OKITA-SENSEI.
DID YOU KNOW ABOUT THAT?
SHE WASN'T HISHIYA'S REAL WIFE...
THE APPRENTICE THAT ACCOM-PANIED HER HAD CALLED HER "OUME-SAN," SO...
I WAS SUSPICIOUS.

IF SHE WAS THE TRUE WIFE, THEN THE PEOPLE AT THE STORE WOULD HAVE CALLED HER "OKU-SAMA."
AND, NO MATTER HOW DESPERATE HISHIYA WAS, I DON'T THINK HE WOULD HAVE SENT HIS WIFE OUT TO SEDUCE SERIZAWA-SENSEI.
...THIS MATTER ABOUT SERIZAWA-SENSEI...
I ASK YOU TO KEEP THIS TO YOUR-SELF.
THERE'S NOTHING GOOD THAT CAN COME BY SERIZAWA-SENSEI KNOWING.
OF COURSE!
NOW...
WHAT?

SERIZAWA-SENSEI AND COMPANY HAVE DISAPPEARED!

YOU THINK IT'S ALL RIGHT WITHOUT SAYING ANYTHING TO OKITA AND KAMIYA...?

WHAT ARE YOU SAYING, SERIZAWA-SENSEI!?

THEY WERE THE INSOLENTS WHO LEFT **AFTER** TAKING US OUT!!

I CAN'T SATISFY MY ANGER UNLESS I BUY A WOMAN.

A WOMAN ...

HH

I KNOW! I CAN'T BE WASTING TIME HERE!
I HAVE TO HURRY AND GET THE 30 *RYO*.
I TOLD OUME THAT I WOULD PAY HER TOMORROW.
SERIZAWA-SENSEI!?
YOU NEED NOT WORRY.
GO AND HAVE A GOOD TIME.
I'M GOING TO GO RAISE SOME MONEY.
SEE YOU LATER!
RIGHT ...
...Are you serious ...?
...OKITA-SENSEI.
THEY'RE DEFINITELY EITHER IN GION OR MIYAKAWA-CHO.
DON'T YOU THINK WE SHOULD GO TO THE BROTHELS INSTEAD OF THE MERCHANTS ...?

I THOUGHT HE WOULD BE GETTING LOANS INSTEAD OF PLAYING AROUND.
HE DID TELL OUME-SAN THAT HE WOULD RETURN THE MONEY TOMORROW.
I SEE.
I HEARD THAT HE SHOOED OFF THE MALE CLERKS INSISTING HE WAS "BUSY."
THREE TIMES.
dancing a little
WHAT ARE YOU SO UPSET ABOUT?
BECAUSE SERIZAWA-SENSEI IS STOOPING SO LOW!!
HA HA HA.
YOU ARE A HARSH ONE, KAMIYA-SAN.
BUT YOU'RE MISTAKING "STOOPING LOW"...
...FOR "FEELING LONELY."

...!

SERIZAWA-
SENSEI...!!

SERI-ZAWA-SENSEI.

-----

ha...

WHA?!

W-WHAT ARE YOU DOING HERE, OKITA?

LET'S GO HOME.

NO, NO, NO, NO, I-I'VE STILL GOT TO BORROW MONEY.
I JUST HAPPENED TO PASS BY HERE, KAMIYA.

HEH
SHALL WE GO HOME, SENSEI?

IF YOU SETTLE YOUR BILL...
THEN YOU WON'T BE ABLE TO SEE OUME-SAN AFTER TOMORROW.
HA
!!
K-KAMIYA, OKITA...
YOU HAVE IT ALL WRONG!
IT-IT-IT'S NOT LIKE I'VE FALLEN FOR ANOTHER MAN'S WIFE...
YES, YES, WE KNOW! ♡
SEI LOOKED AT THE MAN WHO SAID "SHE LOOKS LIKE MY SISTER-IN-LAW"...
...MAKING PETTY EXCUSES...
...AND FELT A FONDNESS FOR HIM FOR THE FIRST TIME.

SERIZAWA-SENSEI IS IN LOVE?!
I'M TELLING YOU, KONDO-SENSEI.
HER NAME IS OUME-SAN, AND SHE'S THE PRETTY WIFE OF HISHIYA, THE FUTOMONO STORE-KEEPER.

AHAHAHAHA
KAMO TOOK A FANCY TO OUME... NOW THAT'S A GOOD LAUGH! ※
I DON'T UNDER-STAND WHAT'S SO FUNNY...
SERIZAWA-SENSEI IS *VERY* SERIOUS.

※ Ume: plum; Kamo: goose

I'll tell everyone what happened when you were 17 if you don't lighten up.
Don't be shy.

"TA" TATEITA NI MIZU "TO SPEAK NINE WORDS AT ONCE"

SOJI...
YOU'RE NOT SAYING THAT HE ATTACKED HER OR ANYTHING, RIGHT?
OF COURSE NOT!
SERIZAWA-SENSEI WOULD NEVER DO SOMETHING LIKE THAT.
I THINK YOU-KNOW-WHO IS MUCH QUICKER WITH THE WOMEN.
TWITCH
"YOU-KNOW-WHO"...?! WHO THE HELL ARE YOU TALKING ABOUT, SOJI?!
WELL, IT'S ONLY A RUMOR BUT... I HEARD THAT THERE WAS SOME GUY WHO KNOCKED UP A WOMAN WHILE IN SERVICE AND GOT KICKED OUT...AND HE WAS ONLY 17...
he he
SHE WAS THE ONE WHO...
WHY THE HELL DOES SOJI KNOW ABOUT THIS?!
THAT WAS BEFORE HE JOINED THE TROOP, KONDO-SAN!!!
So sorry Toshi...it just slipped out...
OH MY GOODNESS... IT WAS ABOUT YOU, HIJIKATA-SAN?!
KNOCK
HAHAHAHAHEHE
CRASH
GET UP!
LIKE YOU DIDN'T KNOW ALL ALONG!

SO ...
I KNOW YOU DIDN'T JUST COME TELL US FOR NO PARTICULAR REASON.
IS THIS OUME GIRL TROUBLE?
COULDN'T SAY...
IT JUST SEEMS THAT SHE'S NOT HISHIYA'S REAL WIFE.
HIS MISTRESS?

THEN IT REALLY DOESN'T MATTER.
WHO CARES IF KAMO HAS HIS WICKED WAY WITH HER.
Hmmf
wait a second
IT'S NOT LIKE I DIDN'T NOTICE BEFORE, BUT...
YOU REALLY ARE A WOMAN'S WORST NIGHTMARE...

I'M JUST CONCERNED THAT...
SERIZAWA-SENSEI'S SERIOUS.

HAAA-
AAA...
THERE'S NO NEED FOR SUCH A GLOOMY FACE, SERIZAWA-SENSEI.
YOU SHOULDN'T FORGET TO SMILE!
KAMIYA-A-A-A.
YOU THINK OUME WILL BE MAD THAT I'M GOING TO BREAK MY PROMISE OF PAYING HER 30 *RYO*...?
BAM
IT'S NOT LIKE YOU'RE NOT GOING TO PAY HER. YOU'RE JUST PAYING HER THREE *RYO* OF IT TODAY.
HERE YOU GO.
WHAT'S THIS MOUNTAIN OF CHANGE?
IT'S THE THREE *RYO* OKITA-SENSEI AND I BORROWED FROM THE MEN.

※*kinka*: Literally, "gold money," *kinka* was the currency of highly ranked bushi. Lowly ranked bushi used *ginka*, or "silver money." The exchange rate changed, but during the Bunkyu era, one *ryo* of *kinka* was equal to 8,000 to 9,000 mon.

YOU EXPECT ME TO LOOK LIKE A POOR FOOL?!

A RIGHTFUL BUSHI SHOULD PAY WITH **KINKA**※ ...

SERIZAWA-SENSEI, IT'S SILLY TO PLAY THE BUSHI CARD WITH MERCHANTS.

A.N.D.

YOU SHOULD SAY SOME-THING LIKE...

"I CANNOT ALLOW MYSELF TO MAKE YOU CARRY HOME SOMETHING SO HEAVY WITH YOUR FRAGILE ARMS"—TO HIDE YOUR ULTERIOR MOTIVE BEHIND NOT COLLECTING THE ENTIRE 30 *RYO* SO YOU COULD SEE HER AGAIN. ♡

Y-YOU HAVE A POINT...

Wha!

NO!!

YOU'RE WRONG... YOU'RE WRONG, KAMIYA!

I DON'T HAVE ANY ULTERIOR MOTIVES! SHE'S ANOTHER MAN'S WIFE!

OH, THAT'S RIGHT.

I FORGOT.

YOUR WANTING TO SEE A BEAUTIFUL PLUM FLOWER...

...SHOULDN'T BE CALLED AN "ULTERIOR MOTIVE."

EXCUSE MY IMPERTI-NENCE!

BUT SUCH A GOOD-HEARTED CHILD HE IS...
SERIZAWA-SENSEI, WHAT TOWN SHOULD WE PATROL TODAY?

OH, IT'S YOU NI'IMI...
UH... I DON'T MUCH FEEL LIKE GOING.
WHY DON'T YOU GO AHEAD AND HAVE FUN.
...

I CAN'T BELIEVE HOW ADORABLE SERIZAWA-SENSEI IS! ♡
WHEN-EVER YOU TALK ABOUT OUME-SAN, HE GETS RED TO HIS EARS!
だんご

Sign: Dumplings

I HOPE YOU'RE NOT AGITATING MATTERS, KAMIYA-SAN.
This must be dealt with in confidence...
OH NO...
IT'S JUST THAT HIS DEDICATION MAKES ME WANT TO HELP OUT. ♡
AND SINCE SHE'S NOT REALLY A MARRIED WOMAN, WE DON'T HAVE TO MAKE HIM GIVE UP... SO THERE'S STILL SOME HOPE...
KAMIYA-SAN!
PLEASE DON'T DO HIM ANY UN-NECESSARY FAVORS.
IT'S NOT A MATTER THAT A CHILD CAN UNDER-STAND.
CHILD...?

I MEAN, THAT WASN'T WHAT I MEANT ...
I'M NOT SAYING YOU'RE A CHILD... I'M JUST... SAYING THAT MATTERS OF THE HEART ARE DELICATE...
EVEN I KNOW SOMETHING ABOUT LOVE!!
HUH?
EVEN I'VE EXPERIENCED...
...AN ACHING HEART ...!!
OH, THAT'S RIGHT.
YOU HAVE A LOVELY LOVER NAMED AKESATO ...
SMASH
!!
OUWWWWW
KEEP LAUGHING, CLOWN-BOY!!

HE COMPLETELY... UTTERLY... THINKS OF ME AS A CHILD!!

GOD, YOU JUST CAN'T KEEP YOUR HANDS TO YOURSELF!

YOU HAVE YOUR WIFE AND OUME-HAN, AND YOU'RE STILL NOT SATISFIED?!

DON'T BE SILLY... THOSE OLD HAGS—

I'M TELLING YOU THAT YOU'RE THE ONLY ONE FOR ME! ♡

?!

SERIZAWA-SENSEI HAS SO MUCH MORE TO OFFER THAN THAT PERVERT...
SERIZAWA-SENSEI!!
HM?
WHAT HAPPENED?
I WANTED TO TALK TO YOU ABOUT HISHIYA...
OUME-SAN'S ACTUALLY...
"PLEASE DON'T DO HIM ANY UNNECESSARY FAVORS..."
NO, I'M DOING THE RIGHT THING!
I'M NOT A CHILD ANYMORE.
THERE IS SOMETHING THAT I THOUGHT YOU SHOULD KNOW!
I'M CAPABLE OF JUDGING WHAT I SHOULD OR SHOULDN'T SAY!
OUME-SAN ISN'T ACTUALLY HISHIYA'S WIFE...

SHE'S HIS MISTRESS?!
AND HE HAS OTHER MIS-TRESSES!
SENSEI, THERE'S NO REASON FOR YOU TO HOLD BACK!
YOU SHOULD REALLY PURSUE HER... THINK OF HER HAPPINESS!!
I, KAMIYA SEIZABURO, WILL BE AT YOUR DISPOSAL!!
A MIS-TRESS ...
SUCH A BEAUTIFUL WOMAN...
IS FORCED TO LIVE IN THE SHADOWS ...?
SO I'M SAY-ING...
YOU SHOULD BECOME HER SUN.
I SEE ...

YOU'RE ABSOLUTELY RIGHT, KAMIYA!!
I'M BEGINNING TO FEEL REALLY GOOD ABOUT THIS!!
THAT'S THE SPIRIT!!
WELL, I HAVE TO GO ON PATROL NOW, SO...
THE BEST OF LUCK TO YOU!!
RIGHT!!
I'M SUPPOSED TO BECOME OUME'S SUN, HUH?
HE HAS SUCH A KNACK WITH WORDS... WHAT A FITTING DESCRIPTION OF ME.
HUM
PARDON ME.
!!
BA-BUMP
!!
O-OUME-DONO!

I HEARD AT THE MAIN HOUSE THAT YOU WERE OVER HERE, BUT...
I'M SORRY. IS THIS A BAD TIME?
N-NO.
D-D-DON'T WORRY.
IT'S HOT OUTSIDE.
P-P-PLEASE COME IN.
WHY THANK YOU.
ANYTHING OUT OF ORDER MACHIDOSHIYORI-SAN※?
GOOD AFTERNOON.
YOU'RE ALWAYS HARD AT WORK, KAMIYA-SAN.
WHERE'S OKITA-SENSEI TODAY?

※ *Machidoshiyori*: Literally, "town's elderly." A town's representative who took care of residents' and official town business.

I'M HERE, JUST TRYING TO KEEP UP...
I DON'T KNOW WHERE KAMIYA-SAN GETS HIS ENERGY IN THIS WEATHER.
HA HA, I SEE.
WHY DON'T YOU STAY AND TAKE A BREAK?

WE HAVEN'T BEEN BOTHERING YOU RECENTLY, HAVE WE?
YOU'RE REFER-RING TO SERIZAWA-SENSEI?
NOT AROUND HERE, THANKS TO YOU.
BUT, I HAVE HEARD THAT THERE'S BEEN SOME TROUBLE OVER AT HISHIYA'S OF HORIKAWA...
OH, DON'T WORRY ABOUT THAT. IT'S ALREADY TAKEN CARE OF!

KAMIYA-SAN?
SERIZAWA-SENSEI CAN BE PUSHY AT TIMES, BUT...
I BELIEVE THAT A SPECIAL SOMEBODY CAN TURN HIM AROUND.

...KAMIYA-SAN!
WHAT HAVE YOU DONE?!
OW!
WHY ARE YOU SO UPSET?
DON'T YOU AGREE?
DON'T YOU THINK THAT IF OUME-SAN AND SERIZAWA-SENSEI HIT IT OFF...
TELL ME!
WHAT DID YOU DO?!
I TOLD HIM THAT OUME-SAN WAS HISHIYA'S MISTRESS, BUT... WHY?
!

PLEASE CONTINUE WITH THE PATROL AFTER YOU ALL FINISH YOUR BREAK!
I'LL MEET UP WITH YOU LATER!
OKITA-SENSEI?!
WHY?!
WHAT'S GOING ON...?!
YOU HAVEN'T A CLUE!!
YOU HAVE NO IDEA...
WHAT KIND OF MAN SERIZAWA-SENSEI IS...
OR WHAT A **MAN** EVEN IS!!
WHAT ...?

JINGLE
THIS IS...?
IT... IT'S THREE RYO.
SERIZAWA-SENSEI...
ARE YOU PULLING MY LEG?
THE BILL WAS FOR 30 RYO...
Y... YES... I UNDERSTAND, BUT...
I... I DIDN'T WANT IT TO BE BURDENSOME FOR YOU.
IS THIS DRUNK HALLUCINATING?
YOU ARE TOO KIND, SERIZAWA-SENSEI.
BUT IF I DON'T BRING HOME 30 RYO TODAY...
YOU DON'T KNOW HOW BADLY MY HUSBAND WILL SCOLD ME.

"HUS-BAND" ?!
IS THERE ANY WAY...?
I BESEECH YOU, SERI-ZAWA-SENSEI.
THINK OF IT AS SAVING ME...
BUMP
...OUME-DONO...
DID YOUR HUSBAND TELL YOU...
TO BEG LIKE THIS AS WELL...?
HUH?

I WOULD NEVER... LET MY DEAREST ...
MY BEAUTIFUL AND DEAREST LADY....
I WOULD NEVER ALLOW HER TO BEG IN FRONT OF A SCOUNDREL WITH A POOR REPUTATION!!
SERIZAWA-SENSEI...
SENSEI, PLEASE, MY HAND ...
I HAVE A HUSBAND.
YOU NEEDN'T LIE TO ME!
I KNOW THAT HISHIYA IS THE KIND OF MAN WHO FORGETS YOU IN THE SHADOWS!
!
OUME, PLEASE BE MINE!
I PROMISE I'LL TAKE CARE OF YOU! I'LL TAKE MUCH BETTER CARE OF YOU THAN HISHIYA EVER COULD!!

STOP!
LET GO OF ME!
OUME.
NO!
WHO WOULD EVER... WITH A MAN LIKE YOU...
HISHIYA HAS OTHER WOMEN!!
...!
YOU THINK I DON'T KNOW THAT ...?!

OKITA-SENSEI!
WA—
PLEASE WAIT...
...OUME-SAN...!
!!
huff
huff
huff

O... OUME-SA...
DON'T TOUCH ME!
WHAT ...
IS ANYONE HERE?
PLEASE CALL A CARRIAGE FOR HER!
DOES THIS MEAN?
THERE'S NO WAY...
...SERIZAWA-SENSEI COULD...?!

IT'S OVER...
OUME WILL NEVER COME BACK...
WH... WHAT HAVE YOU DONE ...!
SERI-ZAWA-SEN...!!
GRAB
YOU HAVE NO RIGHT TO ACCUSE HIM OF ANYTHING!
BUT...
I NEVER THOUGHT THAT HE WAS CAPABLE OF DOING SOMETHING SO ATROCIOUS ...!!

ATROCIOUS?!
SERIZAWA-SENSEI WAS SERIOUS!!
HOW ELSE DID YOU EXPECT HIM TO ACT?!

HE CAN'T STOP HIMSELF BECAUSE HE'S ALL HEART AND SOUL, AND HE'S SO SERIOUS, AND SO AWKWARD...
YOU'RE THE ONE WHO KNOWINGLY UNLEASHED HIM ON HER!!

HE'S RIGHT...
I'M THE ONE TO BLAME...

CAN'T BE STOPPED BY ANYONE NOW.

HELP
WHAT KIND OF WAITRESS ARE YOU!
WHY DO YOU LOOK AT ME LIKE I'M SOME KIND OF ANIMAL!
DID YOU HEAR THAT SERIZAWA OF THE MIBU-RO CAUSED A RUCKUS AT THE RESTAURANT BY SHIMABARA AND CAUSED THEM TO STOP BUSINESS FOR SEVEN DAYS?!
SHH!!
WHAT IF SOMEONE HEARS YOU?
I HEARD THAT SOMEONE GOT THEIR HEAD CUT OFF BECAUSE THEY TALKED BADLY ABOUT HIM!
RAW SILK MERCHANT YAMATO-YA!
YOU ARE GUILTY OF RAISING PRICES BY BUYING OUT THE MARKET AND PROVIDING THE SONJO-HA WITH FUNDS!!
I, CAPTAIN SERIZAWA KAMO OF THE MIBU-ROSHI, WILL DISPOSE OF YOU!!

RRRRRRRRRRRR
SERIZAWA IS BURNING THE MERCHANT'S STORE?!
HE'S LOST IT!
IS HE POSSESSED BY A DEMON?!
...IT'S MY RESPONSIBILITY.
HA HA HA HA! IT'S A DIRECT ORDER FROM THE CAPTAIN! BURN! BURN!
BURN EVERYTHING!!
SERIZAWA-SENSEI—PLEASE STOP!
IT'S GONE TOO FAR!!

SMACK!!
SHUT UP!
Kamiya-sa...
BAM

I...I'M SORRY ...
HA HA HA, YOU IDIOTS!
You ok?
AND YOU THOUGHT YOU WERE HIS FAVORITE ...
THAT IS THE TRUE SERIZAWA KAMO!
WEREN'T YOU HOPING TO LEARN SOME-THING SPECIAL BY FOLLOWING HIS EXAMPLE?
HA HA HA HA HA HA

THESE PEOPLE...
HAVE THEY BEEN FOLLOWING SERIZAWA-SENSEI FOR SOMETHING SO PETTY...?
...!

GRAB
KAMI-YA?!
WHAT ARE YOU DOING? YOU'RE HURT...
HARADA-SAN!
LET HIM GO.
THIS IS SOME-THING THAT KAMIYA-SAN HAS TO TAKE CARE OF HIMSELF.
GULP GULP GULP
SERI-ZAWA-SENSEI!
THIS MAN...

...IS TRULY ALL ALONE.
WHAT THE HELL ARE YOU DOING UP HERE AGAIN?
I'LL COME BACK AS MANY TIMES AS IT TAKES!
BECAUSE I CARE ABOUT YOU!

HMF.
AS IF YOU GAVE A DAMN!
ARE YOU SAYING YOU'LL JOIN MY MITO CLAN?!
IF THAT IS YOUR WISH!
LIAR!!
WHAT IF OKITA...
...ORDERS YOU TO KILL ME?!

HAA HA HA HA, KAMIYA!!
Y-YES?!
I KNOW OF NO ONE...
...AS TRUST-WORTHY AS YOU.
LET'S GO DOWN!

OH MY GOD, OUME!
SERIZAWA'S BURNING YAMATO-YA!
WHAT?!

HE'S A LUNATIC
WHAT AM I GOING TO DO WHEN HE BURNS ME DOWN TOO?!
I KNOW I ASKED A LOT OF YOU, BUT DON'T YOU THINK IT WAS A BAD CALL TO ANGER HIM?

I DON'T CARE ABOUT THE BILL ANYMORE, SO WHY DON'T YOU GO BACK AND APOLOGIZE TO SETTLE MATTERS...
YOU DARE SAY THAT KNOWING VERY WELL WHAT HAPPENED TO ME?!

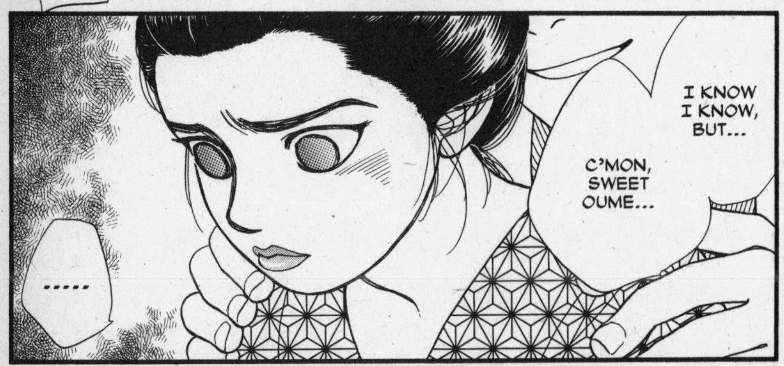
I KNOW I KNOW, BUT...
C'MON, SWEET OUME...
.....

I'M FINISHED PUNISHING THE NE'ER-DO-WELLS!
WE'RE GOING HOME!
FWIP
OW.
WELL DONE.
OKITA-SENSEI ...!
NOW...
!!

HISHIYA ... I LEFT HIM.
TREAT ME WELL.
THIS WAS THE DAY...
THAT, WITH THE INSTIGATION OF THE SONJO-HA, EMPEROR KOMEI'S YAMATO VISIT TO PRAY FOR EXCLUSION-ISM WAS DECIDED UPON.
THE DAY THAT THE KOBU-GATTAI-HA※ WOULD...
...START WHAT WOULD BE KNOWN AS THE "AUGUST 18TH COUP"...
...WAS A MERE FIVE DAYS AWAY.

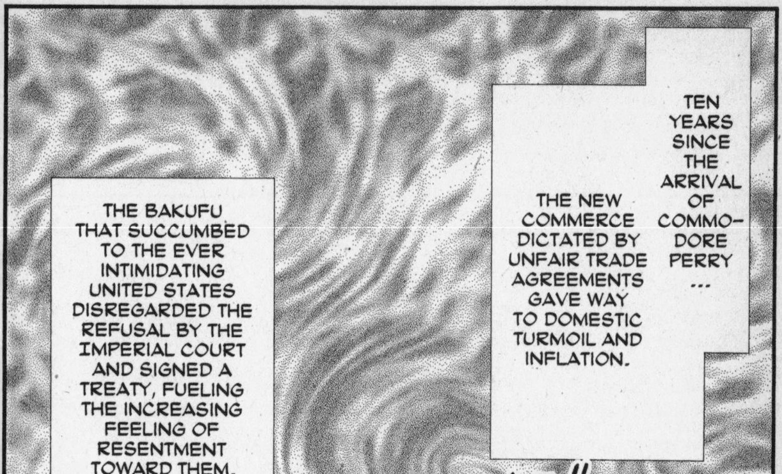

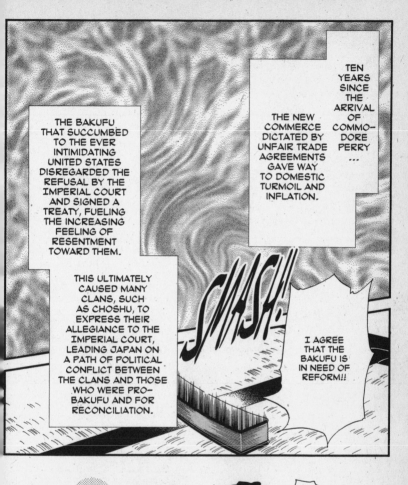

TEN YEARS SINCE THE ARRIVAL OF COMMODORE PERRY...

THE NEW COMMERCE DICTATED BY UNFAIR TRADE AGREEMENTS GAVE WAY TO DOMESTIC TURMOIL AND INFLATION.

THE BAKUFU THAT SUCCUMBED TO THE EVER INTIMIDATING UNITED STATES DISREGARDED THE REFUSAL BY THE IMPERIAL COURT AND SIGNED A TREATY, FUELING THE INCREASING FEELING OF RESENTMENT TOWARD THEM.

THIS ULTIMATELY CAUSED MANY CLANS, SUCH AS CHOSHU, TO EXPRESS THEIR ALLEGIANCE TO THE IMPERIAL COURT, LEADING JAPAN ON A PATH OF POLITICAL CONFLICT BETWEEN THE CLANS AND THOSE WHO WERE PRO-BAKUFU AND FOR RECONCILIATION.

SMASH!!

I AGREE THAT THE BAKUFU IS IN NEED OF REFORM!!

KYOTO "IROHA" KARUTA GAME!
I'm gonna do it!
れ
"RE" RENGI DE HARA O KIRU "TO MAKE A HOLE IN THE WATER"
Just stop while you're ahead.

THOUGH IT IS NOT WITHOUT REASON THAT A WELL FUNDED, WELL ARMED, AND LARGE CLAN SUCH AS CHOSHU ...
HAS VISIONS OF A DIFFERENT COUNTRY...
A COUNTRY WITHOUT A BAKUFU, RUN BY SPINELESS BUSHI WHO CONTRIBUTE NOTHING TO THE *SHOGUNATE*!
BUT GENTLEMEN, THERE *ARE* HEROES ON THE BAKUFU SIDE!
JUST LOOK AT LIEUTENANT GENERAL MATSUDAIRA KATAMORI-SAMA OF HIGO, LORD PROTECTOR OF KYOTO, WHO GRACIOUSLY PROVIDES FOR US!!
FURTHER! IT IS EMPEROR KOMEI'S OWN WISH...
FOR EXCLUSIONISM UPON RECONCILIATION BETWEEN THE IMPERIAL COURT AND THE BAKUFU—
WHAT BETTER TIME THAN NOW FOR THE ABLE AND TRUE BUSHI OF THE MIBU-ROSHI TO REBUILD THE BAKUFU, DEFEAT CHOSHU, AND LEAD THE WAY TO EXCLUSIONISM!!

I DON'T BELIEVE IT! HOW CAN THIS MAN BE THE DRUNKEN FOOL I WITNESSED THE OTHER DAY?
ELOQUENTLY PUT, CAPTAIN!!
ROAR
CLAP CLAP CLAP CLAP
WHY THE SUDDEN CHANGE...?
UH-HUM!
WHAT DID YOU THINK, OUME?
I DIDN'T REALLY UNDER-STAND IT.
DMP
ENOUGH OF THAT. WHEN ARE YOU SUMMON-ING THE TAILOR FOR ME?
I RAN OUT HERE IN MY RAGS BECAUSE YOU SAID YOU WOULD TAKE CARE OF ME.

I KNOW, I KNOW.
I SENT YAGI'S MAID OUT, SO SHE SHOULD BE BACK BEAR-ING GIFTS. ♡
REALLY?! OH, I'M SO EXCITED! ♡
...KAMIYA-SAN...
WHO WAS GOING TO CALM SERIZAWA-SENSEI DOWN AGAIN...?
IT-IT'S GONNA BE ALL RIGHT.
HE'S ALREADY TURNING HIMSELF AROUND...
DIDN'T YOU HEAR HIS SPEECH?!
YOU'RE ONLY SEEING...
WHO SERIZAWA KAMO REALLY IS—
HOT-HEADED AND RATHER PRONE TOWARD VIOLENCE.
HE TRULY WOULD BE A HERO IF HE THOUGHT MATTERS OUT MORE THOROUGHLY AND STOPPED BEING SUCH A VIOLENT DRUNK.
SENSEI...
THAT WOULD ONLY MAKE HIM A THUG.

HEY ... SAITO-SAN'S BACK! ♡
HGH

...
...

...WHAT'S HAPPENED?

OKITA-SEN...

not there

slip

slip

slip

So we are... and

First we must...

NOBODY'S SAID ANYTHING YET.
THEY CAN ALL FEEL SOME-THING IN THE AIR.
THESE EIGHT MEN OF SHIEIKAN...
WHAT AN INCREDIBLE GROUP...
AN ORDER'S BEEN ISSUED FOR THE EMPEROR KOMEI'S YAMATO※ VISIT?!
Lower your voice Toshi...
I UNDER-STAND THAT THE EMPEROR'S PRAYING FOR EXCLU-SIONISM, BUT THIS IS THE THIRD TIME THIS YEAR!
IS THE EMPEROR TRYING TO ASSUME COMMAND OF EXCLU-SIONISM HIMSELF?!
IT SEEMS THAT HE WAS PUSHED BY CHOSHU AND THE NOBLES WHO WISH FOR THE EMPEROR AND EXCLUSIONISM TO THRIVE.

※*Yamato* refers to the present Nara Prefecture.

THEY'RE UP TO SOMETHING!!
THERE'S NO WAY THAT THEY WOULD BRING THE EMPEROR TO YAMATO JUST TO PRAY AT THE KASUGA SHRINE!
I AGREE.
WE'RE TALKING ABOUT THOSE SCUMBAGS. THEY'RE PROBABLY PLANNING ON KIDNAPPING THE EMPEROR OR SOMETHING.
ARE WE GONNA ASK TO ESCORT THE EMPEROR?

BUT EVEN THE BAKUFU ISN'T THAT STUPID.
I CAN'T IMAGINE THAT KATAMORI-SAMA, OR SATSUMA-HAN, HAVE OVER-LOOKED THE SITUATION.
OR EVEN THE NOBLES LOOKING FOR RECON-CILIATION.

WHATEVER THE CASE, IT MEANS BATTLE.
MAKE SURE THAT YOUR SUBORDINATES ARE ALL READY SO THAT WE CAN DEPART IMMEDIATELY WHEN CALLED UPON!

ALL RIGHT!!
TMP TMP TMP
...LOOKS LIKE YOU'RE ALL HAVING A GOOD TIME.
OF COURSE WE'RE HAVING A GOOD TIME!
...I MEAN, WHERE THE HELL HAVE YOU BEEN?!
I'VE BEEN HERE ALL ALONG.
YOU ALWAYS SHY AWAY WHEN STUFF LIKE THIS IS BROUGHT UP.
I DON'T LIKE DEALING WITH DIFFICULT MATTERS.

"DIFFICULT"?! WHAT THE HELL DID YOU COME TO KYOTO FOR?!
TO BABYSIT YOU?
SHUT UP!
HE'S RIGHT, THOUGH...
SMASH
HE HE HE
CRASH
KONDO-SENSEI, KONDO-SENSEI.
SAITO-SAN DIDN'T MENTION ANYTHING ELSE?
POP
OOUP

SOJI.
GET OUT OF HERE!
MAKE SURE YOU GET EVERYBODY TO TAKE CARE OF THEIR WEAPONS AND EQUIPMENT!
I KNOW.
"CAPTAIN KONDO AND BOTH VICE-CAPTAINS, HIJIKATA AND YAMANAMI, ARE ORDERED TO COME TO KURODANI※ HEADQUARTERS IN CONFIDENCE TONIGHT..."
IT'S AN ORDER FROM KATAMORI-SAMA.
SAITO-KUN WAS TOLD TO REPORT THIS IN SECRECY.
I DON'T KNOW WHY HE'S SO KEEN ON THINGS.
"IN CONFI-DENCE"...
...I WONDER WHAT HE WANTS.
WELL...
JUDGING FROM THE FACT THAT SERIZAWA WASN'T CALLED UPON...
I DOUBT HE WANTS TO JUST GIVE A LECTURE.

※The Kyoto Protectors used Konkai Komyo Temple as their headquarters, which was commonly referred to as *Kurodani*.

PUT COTTON ON THE INSIDE OF THE *HACHIGANE*,※ WRAP IT AROUND WITH A SASH, AND SEW IT.
ADJUST THE AMOUNT OF COTTON YOU USE BY HOW IT FEELS ON YOUR FOREHEAD.
FEEL IT WITH YOUR FINGERS.
SEE HOW THERE'RE HOLES? SEW IT THROUGH THERE.
YOU'RE SO GOOD WITH YOUR HANDS, KAMIYA.
WILL YOU DO MINE TOO? ♡
ME TOO! ♡
MINE TOO! ♡
YOU WORTH-LESS...
WE'RE GOING TO WAR!
This is good.

※*hachigane*: armor to protect the forehead.

THE KOZUKA※ AND THE KOGAI WILL BOTH GET IN THE WAY.
THE SLIT FOR THEM WEAKENS MY SCAB-BARD...
they're put right here
"WHY DID YOU HAVE IT MADE WITH A KOGAI?"
"WELL, BECAUSE ..."
...
Grip
!!
?
He He
no other intentions
"YOU'RE A GIRL ..." (ECHOING)
I'M GONNA FILL THE SLIT!!
I'M NOT A GIRL, AND I NEVER USE A KOGAI!!
WH-WHY ALL OF THE SUDDEN?!

※ A *kozuka* is a decorative miniature katana, which, like the *kogai*, serves no purpose in battle.

Yagi Family's Main House
YOU REALLY ARE GOOD WITH YOUR HANDS.
YOU CAN'T EVEN TELL THAT THERE WAS A SLIT NOW THAT YOU PACKED AND PAINTED IT.
HA HA HA!
THANKS FOR YOUR PAINT, TAMEBO AND YUBO.
YOU'RE SO STUBBORN.
THANK YOU VERY MUCH.
THANK YOU FOR YOUR TROUBLES.
THAT'S THE OBI※ MERCHANT FROM SHINMACHI.
SOMEONE'S HERE ALL THE TIME THESE DAYS. SERIZAWA JUST DOES WHAT OUME TELLS HIM TO DO. CALL THE TAILOR, THE ACCESSORY MERCHANT, THE SHOE MERCHANT...
...
Annex to the house
GOOD-NESS OUME...
YOU LOOK STUNNING! ♡
Spoony
Spoony
REALLY? THANKS.

※*Obi:* an elaborate sash worn with a kimono

...I'LL HAVE A WORD WITH HIM...!
NO YOU WILL NOT.

HE WILL NOT HESITATE TO KILL YOU.

...

I CHOKED ON MY WORDS ...

...THE NIGHT OF THE FIRE ON THE ROOF.

HAD HE STRUCK ME WITH HIS METAL FAN HEAD-ON, I WOULD NOT BE BREATHING RIGHT NOW.

I SURVIVED ONLY BECAUSE ...
...I PULLED BACK AND FELL.
IF SOMEONE WERE TO...
...SPEAK ILL OF HIS BELOVED, WHO HE MIRACULOUSLY WON...
...WHO KNOWS WHAT HE IS CAPABLE OF...
WAS THIS LOVE ...
...SOME-THING THAT SHOULD HAVE BEEN FORBIDDEN?
WHAT THE HELL ARE YOU DOING!
I WANT MORE WOMEN!!
AND SAKE!!

CALL THE TAILOR WHILE YOU'RE AT IT.
I'LL HAVE KIMONOS MADE FOR ALL OF YOU.
REALLY, NI'IMI-SENSEI!?
PUT IT ON CAPTAIN SERIZAWA KAMO OF THE MIBU-ROSHI'S TAB!
AFTER ALL, HE'S THE ONE WHO TOLD US TO GO OUT AND HAVE FUN!
HAHAHAHAH
COME TO THINK OF IT, HE HASN'T BEEN AROUND LATELY.
THAT'S BECAUSE A PRETTY GIRL NAMED OUME HAS HIM ON A TIGHT LEASH.
SO, NO MORE OF THE OLD SERIZAWA...
BO-RING!!
VICE-CAPTAIN NI'IMI...
CAPTAIN KONDO REQUESTS YOUR RETURN...
SHUT UP!
I DON'T REMEMBER BEING UNDER KONDO'S COMMAND!!

...WHAT OMINOUS CLOUDS ...
COULDN'T SLEEP EITHER?
NO...
I HAVE A BAD FEELING ...
OKITA-SENSEI! SAITO-SENSEI!
IT'S A MESSENGER FROM AIZU—
REQUESTING CAPTAIN KONDO'S AUDIENCE!
EVERY-BODY UP!
GET UP!!
Klack Klack

IT'S TIME!!
THE THIRD YEAR OF BUNKYU (1863) BEFORE THE DAWN OF AUGUST 18TH.
AIZU AND SATSUMA JOINED FORCES WITH NAKAGAWANOMIYA AND OTHER KOBUGATTAI-HA WITHIN THE COURT. THEY STAGED A COUP D'ÉTAT WHEREIN THE EXTENSION OF THE YAMATO VISIT AND THE EXILE OF THE *SONJO-HA* NOBLES AND CHOSHU WERE DEMANDED.
THIS MARKED THE BEGINNING OF WHAT CAME TO BE KNOWN AS THE "AUGUST 18TH COUP."
I ASSUME YOU ARE ALL PREPARED!!
YEAHHH
WE SHALL DEPART TO PROTECT THE EMPEROR!

OUME—
I MAY NOT RETURN.
BUT IF I MAY DIE PROTECTING THE LORD EMPEROR, I'LL HAVE NO REGRETS.
SO DO NOT BE SADDENED.
RIGHT. WHAT-EVER.
B'BYE...
YOU'LL SEE!
I WILL COME BACK TO YOU A DECORATED HERO!!
WE ARE MEMBERS OF THE MIBU-ROSHI, SERVING THE LORD OF AIZU!
WE ARE HERE TO SERVE AND PROTECT THE COURT BY ORDER OF OUR CLAN.
OPEN THE GATES!

OUTE GATES OF TH COUR (HAMA GURI-MON)
DON'T BE RIDICU-LOUS!
I WAS NOT NOTIFIED!
GO HOME!
WHAT?!
I DON'T UNDER-STAND?
GET OUT OF MY WAY, YOU IMBECILE!!
YOU WILL REGRET YOUR DISCOUR-TESY!
I AM A MAN OF LOYALTY AND PATRIOTISM— CAPTAIN SERIZAWA KAMO OF THE MIBU-ROSHI!!

IF YOU DO NOT OPEN THESE GATES, I WILL TEAR THEM DOWN BY FORCE!!
ULP
S-SERI-ZAWA-SENSEI?!
RAAAAA
THAT IDIOT ...!!
STOP HIM, SOJI!
YES, BUT...
LOOK, HIJIKATA-SAN

HE REALLY IS A MAN OF REMARKABLE SKILL.
HE'S DODGING ALL THOSE SPEARS WITH ONLY HIS METAL FAN IN HAND, AND WHILE WEARING ALL THAT HEAVY ARMOR...
THIS IS NO TIME TO BE IMPRESSED!!
YOU'RE RIGHT.
SERIZAWA-SENSEI, PLEASE STOP!
YOU'RE IN MY WAY!
GET OUT, KAMIYA-A-A-A!!
BAMM

KAMIYA-SAN!
UH... I'M ALL RIGHT.
IT JUST HIT MY *HACHI-GANE*.
WHAT IS GOING ON HERE!!
OH, IT'S AN AIZU OFFICIAL, NOMURA-DONO!
KONDO-UJI?!
HOW CAN YOU BE HERE?! THE ORDER WENT OUT JUST A MOMENT AGO...
YET THE ***ENTIRE*** MIBU-ROSHI IS HERE?!
OF COURSE...
THEY SAY THAT "GODLY SPEED MERITS A SOLDIER."
WHAT INCREDIBLE MEN...!
I AM ASHAMED AND HUMBLY APOLOGIZE FOR MY DISCOURTESY.

OPEN THE GATES!
THE MIBU-ROSHI IS TO GO TO THE FRONT OF THE MAIN GATE!!
I CAN FEEL MYSELF SHAKING ...
TO THINK THAT I WILL BE PROTECT-ING THE EMPEROR ...
誠
TO WHOM I NEVER THOUGHT I WOULD BE OF ANY USE...!!
I'M SO GLAD I BECAME BUSHI!
MOTHER, ARE YOU LOOKING DOWN RIGHT NOW?
THIS IS THE MOST AMAZING THING THAT'S EVER HAPPENED TO ME!

FROM HERE ON OUT, WE SHALL WORK TWICE AS HARD AS ANYONE ELSE...

...AND GIVE OUR LIVES TO BATTLE!!

I'M IN!!

DESPITE THEIR ENTHUSIASM...

THE SURPRISED CHOSHU SIMPLY RETREATED FROM THE PROTECTED GATE OF SAKAI MACHI AFTER A BRIEF STANDOFF WITH THE JOINT FORCES OF AIZU AND SATSUMA.

THE COUP D'ÉTAT ENDED WITH CHOSHU AND SEVEN SONJO-HA NOBLES BEING CHASED OUT OF KYOTO. ALL OF THIS TRANSPIRED OUT OF THE MIBU-ROSHI'S REACH.

...WHO'S GONNA TELL THEM IT'S OVER?
READY TO GO!!
誠

HOWEVER, THE MIBU-ROSHI'S SPEED AND ACTION DID NOT GO UNRECOGNIZED.
AS A RESULT, THEY WERE GIVEN AN OFFICIAL TROOP NAME THAT DAY BY THE *EMPEROR AND NOBLE FAMILIES.*
SHINSENGUMI
...HOWEVER, THE NAME WAS REALLY GIVEN BY KATAMORI OF AIZU.
THE EMPEROR HAS GIVEN US A NAME...
WHAT AN HONOR!!
OH, OUME!
SO AS NOT TO INJURE THEIR PRIDE...
OR ELSE, WHO KNOWS WHAT THEY'D DO.
not relevant
SHINSEN-GUMI.
WHAT AN HONOR-ABLE NAME.
御預 新選

THIRTY YEARS SINCE I WAS BORN A FARMER'S SON IN TAMA...
I NEVER THOUGHT I WOULD RECEIVE A NAME FROM THE EMPEROR.
IT'S A DREAM COME TRUE FOR YOU, SENSEI!
松平肥後守御預
新選組
STOP CRYING, YOU'RE MAKING A FOOL OF YOURSELF!
...WE MUST BECOME WORTHY OF THIS NAME.
WE MUST CREATE A GROUP OF WARRIORS THAT...
...WILL BE UNMATCHED IN JAPAN!
I'LL DO EVERY-THING I CAN!
ME...
ME TOO!!
I MAY NOT BE MUCH, BUT PLEASE LET ME CONTRIBUTE!!

DAMN, KAMIYA STOLE MY THUNDER!
HAHAHAHAHAHAHA
WITH THIS NAME ...
Did I do it again?
oops.
THE LOOSE ORDER OF THIS PARTY MUST BE REFORMED.
THOSE WHO DIS-GRACE OUR NAME...
...WILL BE ELIMINATED!
NI'IMI-SENSEI, YOUR RIDE HAS ARRIVED.
山乃緒
山乃緒

WHAT ARE YOU DOING HERE, OKITA?!
VICE-CAPTAIN NI'IMI...
YOU ARE CHARGED WITH GROSS DEBAUCHERY, EXTORTION IN THE NAME OF CAPTAIN SERIZAWA, AND DERELICTION OF DUTY.
PLEASE RETURN IMMEDIATELY SO THAT WE MAY CARRY OUT AN INVESTIGATION REGARDING THIS MATTER.
AN INVESTIGATION?! YOU BASTARD!!
EVERYTHING WAS APPROVED BY CAPTAIN SERIZAWA! YOU HAVE NO RIGHT TO CHARGE ME!!
GET OUT OF MY SIGHT!
...PLEASE ...
I BEG YOU TO NOT DISGRACE SERIZAWA-SENSEI ANYMORE...

I ASK YOU ...
...TO ACT AS BUSHI.
WHA—
SO I SHOULD RETURN!!
GIVE ME A MOMENT!!
KAMIYA-SAN...
PLEASE CALL FOR THE CARRIAGE.
YES, SIR!
OKI-!

SHING
KAMIYA-SAN, CLOSE THE DOOR!
Y-YES!

SHPA
GRIP
STAB...
...!!
...
PLEASE DO NOT MENTION WHAT YOU JUST WITNESSED.

PLEASE REPORT THAT NI'IMI-SENSEI TOOK HIS LIFE LIKE A BUSHI AND THAT I ASSISTED HIM.
WH... WHY MUST WE LIE...?
YOU'VE DONE NO WRONG.

I DON'T WANT SERIZAWA-SENSEI TO BE SADDENED BY THIS.

WHY NI'IMI?!
WHY DID YOU DO THIS?!
HE SAID THAT HE WANTED TO GO IN GOOD GRACE, TO PAY FOR THE DEBTS OF OVER 200 *RYO* HE RACKED UP IN YOUR NAME...

I SEE... YOU WERE A TRUE BUSHI, NI'IMI...
BUT TOO EARNEST... I WOULD NOT HAVE MINDED A MERE 200 RYO...
YOU SHOULD!!
ALL THAT WOULD HAVE MEANT WAS THAT I NEEDED TO SHOW THAT WORTH IN DUTY.
THEN, PEOPLE WOULD HAVE BEEN PROUD TO HAVE BEEN ABLE TO CONTRIBUTE TO A HERO.
...
...EVEN THOUGH I THINK OF SERIZAWA-SENSEI...
...AS AN OUTRAGEOUS MAN...
...WHY IS IT THAT HE CONVINCES ME...
...OF HIS WAYS SOMETIMES?
IT'S BECAUSE HE'S BUSHI.

EVEN IF ONE MAY NOT AGREE ...

...HE STRICTLY FOLLOWS HIS OWN SAMURAI SPIRIT.

HE DOESN'T BLAME ANYBODY OR MAKE ANY EXCUSES.

THOSE ARE QUALITIES THAT I ADMIRE.

HUH...

SLIP

"I ADMIRE ..."

BAH-BUMP

DEBO-CHIN.
FLIP

I HEARD THAT'S HOW YOU SAY "FOREHEAD" IN KYOTO.
I'M SO HAPPY THAT YOU DIDN'T SCAR.
...I CAN NEVER TAKE YOU SERIOUSLY!!
HAHA HAHA
I LOVE YOU, OKITA-SENSEI.

THAT'S WHY...
I DON'T WANT TO THINK THAT SERIZAWA-SENSEI'S LOVE IS FORBIDDEN.
HOW CAN HE AND OUME-SAN...
LIVE IN BLISS TOGETHER?
OUME! ♡
STUNNING AS ALWAYS! ♡
THEY SAID IT COSTS 120 RYO.
酒
JUST LEAVE IT TO ME.
I'LL BECOME A HERO, AND THEN EVERYBODY WILL WANT TO GIVE ME GIFTS.
IS THIS DRUNK REALLY THIS STUPID?
HIS ANSWER IS ALWAYS THE SAME.
...YOU REALLY LIKE SERIZAWA...
DON'T YOU, SOJI?

YES.
A LOT! ♡
WE MUST KILL HIM.
...
...I UNDERSTAND.

THAT'S ALL YOU HAVE TO SAY?!
AREN'T YOU GOING TO BEG FOR HIS LIFE?! AREN'T YOU GOING TO CURSE MY NAME?!
THANK YOU, HIJIKATA-SAN.
SOJI?
WEREN'T YOU TOLD BY KATAMORI-SAMA...
...TO KEEP THIS STRICTLY CONFIDENTIAL?
WELL ...YES.
BUT WE NEED MORE THAN JUST THE THREE OF US.
WE WERE ORDERED TO "ELIMINATE THE ENTIRE SERIZAWA FACTION."
SO...
I'M THANKING YOU FOR INCLUDING ME.
ARE YOU OUT OF YOUR MIND?!
YOU'RE SO CLOSE TO HIM...!!

To Be Continued!

"SO"
SODESURI
AU MO
TASHO NO EN
"A CHANCE
ACQUAINTANCE
IS PART OF
ONE'S DESTINY"

KYOTO
"IROHA"
KARUTA
GAME

TAEKO WATANABE PRESENTS

KAZE HIKARU

風光る DIARY 2

PLEASE BE SURE TO FINISH READING THE MAIN STORY PORTION BEFORE PROCEEDING FURTHER.

"SEEK SHELTER FROM RAIN" (Not quite sure, but I just thought of it.)

PREVIOUSLY...

"WHAT?! CUSTOMS IN EDO AND KYOTO ARE DIFFERENT?!"

RIGHT.
THEY WERE DIFFERENT.
MATERIALS THEY USED FOR BUILDINGS, AND EVEN THE SHAPE OF THE TOILETS WERE DIFFERENT!
HAIR-STYLES, AND...
...THE WAY THEY MADE THEIR FUTONS TOO?!
...AND THE REASON FOR THE OVERSIGHT WAS...
A film studio in Kyoto.
THE BACK-GROUND (OF KYOTO) IN THE SHINSENGUMI VIDEOS THAT I USED FOR VISUAL REFERENCES WERE THE SAME ONES USED IN OTHER FAMOUS HISTORICAL DRAMAS SET IN EDO...
WHAT?!
SO THAT MEANS THAT...
THE SET AT "UZUMASA" ISN'T A TOWN IN THE "EDO PERIOD," BUT AN "EDO TOWN"?!
OF COURSE THE SAME GOES FOR THE FAMOUS "NIKKO EDO MURA."
MEANING...
Now that I look at it, it's not entirely "Edo" either (heh).

THE OVER 2,000 PICTURES I TOOK AT THOSE TWO LOCATIONS FOR SOURCE DATA ARE ALL WORTHLESS?!
BOOM
16tons

...
SLAM
I'M GONNA PRETEND I NEVER SAW THAT.
Let's get to work.
I'LL BE ALL RIGHT. EVEN THE FILM INDUSTRY'S DOING IT!
NOBODY WILL EVEN NOTICE.

WHO CARES AS LONG AS SO-CHAN IS HOT! ♡
IT'S JUST A SHOJO MANGA...
...
WHO ARE YOU KIDDING?

"IT'LL PROBABLY FEEL A LOT BETTER THAN"...

"...CONTINUING TO DRAW WHILE PRETENDING YOU *DIDN'T* KNOW."

......

DAMN IT!

ALL RIGHT! I GET IT!

YOU WANT ME TO STUDY, RIGHT?
FINE! I'LL DO IT!!
THIS WAS THE FIRST TIME THAT I CAME TO THE REALIZATION THAT THE OVER 30 BOOKS ON THE BOOK-SHELF, COLLECTED TO RESEARCH CUSTOMS OF THE EDO PERIOD, WERE ACTUALLY RESTRICTED GEOGRAPHICALLY TO THE EDO REGION.
写真ネガ
和ろうそく
江戸名所図会
江戸語辞典
江戸の地図
YOU MEAN I HAVE TO START ALL OVER...?!
MAY OF 1997. DISCOURAGED, I WENT ON A RAMPAGE OF BUYING BOOKS THAT INCLUDED "KYO" OR "KAMIGATA" IN THE TITLE, IN SEARCH OF BOOKS ABOUT THE KYOTO REGION.
IT'S AMAZING HOW DIFFERENT KYO AND EDO ARE!!
FROM THE WAY THEY CALL KIMONOS TO EVEN THE WAY THEY LAID OUT SASHIMI...!!
fasci-nating
the assistants
THANKFULLY, THERE WERE MANY BOOKS COMPARING THE TWO CUSTOMS, SO I WAS ABLE TO LEARN A LOT ABOUT EDO AS WELL!!
LOOKING BACK, THIS SHOULD HAVE BEEN THE FIRST ORDER OF BUSINESS.
GOD, I'M LYING ALL OVER THE PLACE!
I've got to fix it before it becomes a book.
TV, MOVIES, NOVELS... ALL FICTION.
IT WAS FOOLISH TO USE THEM AS SOURCE MATERIALS.

THE MORE I UNDER-STOOD ...
THE MORE I REALIZED HOW FRESH AND ELEGANT THE STREETS OF KYOTO WERE.
Look at the lattices!
The roofs are round!

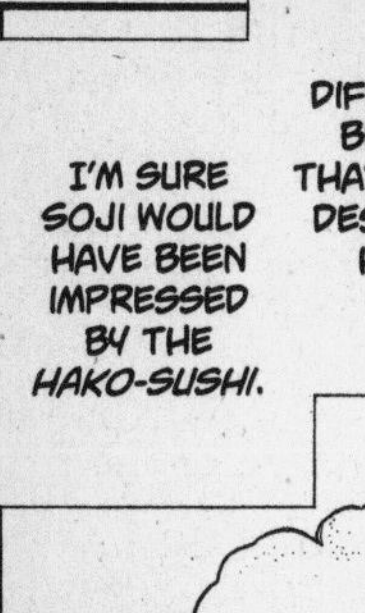
THE DIFFERENT BEAUTY THAT KYOTO DESSERTS HAD...
I'M SURE SOJI WOULD HAVE BEEN IMPRESSED BY THE *HAKO-SUSHI*.
OUUU

THE MORE I LEARNED ABOUT THE DAILY LIVES OF THESE COUNTRY BUSHI FROM EDO ...
LIKE WHAT THEY ATE, HOW THEY SLEPT, AND WHAT KINDS OF THINGS STUNNED THEM OR EVEN TROUBLED THEM...
Oh my god! Look at what that girl's doing on the side of the road!
Oh dear...
The Kyoto natives don't notice.
WAS THE KEY TO BRINGING SOJI AND THE OTHER CHARACTERS TO LIFE.
What do you think they saw? I'm not telling because I'd be spilling the beans on the story (heh).

THIS IS...
...SO INTER-ESTING!!

I HAVE A TENDENCY OF BEING CAPTIVATED BY THE EMOTIONS OF INDIVIDUALS RATHER THAN THE HISTORICAL EVENTS THEMSELVES.
THAT'S RIGHT! I'LL WRITE ABOUT THE "DAILY LIVES" OF THE SHINSENGUMI!! I'LL GO INTO HISTORY FROM THERE!! WHAT DO YOU GUYS THINK? AWESOME, ISN'T IT?!
WHATEVER, WE JUST WANT YOU TO DECIDE ON THESE THINGS BEFORE YOU START THE SERIES.
IT'LL SAVE US FROM HAVING TO GO BACK AND CORRECT THEM.
THAT WAS HOW MY COLLECTION OF HISTORICAL WRITINGS PERTAINING TO CUSTOMS INCREASED TENFOLD, AND...
PRESENTLY, IN AUGUST OF 1998, I EASILY HAVE OVER 300 SOURCE BOOKS.
BUT...
I CAN'T GET THROUGH ALL OF THEM!!
Don't give up!
PLUS, WHY CAN'T I RETAIN ANY OF THIS KNOWLEDGE?!
And why does my head feel so heavy?
THE ROAD AHEAD WILL NOT BE SMOOTH, SO I ASK FOR YOUR SUPPORT!
Even this volume has a ton of corrections
TO BE CONTINUED...
...or not?

Decoding Kaze Hikaru

Kaze Hikaru is a historical drama based in 19th century Japan and thus contains some fairly mystifying terminology. In this glossary we'll break down archaic phrases, terms, and other linguistic curiosities for you so that you can move through life with the smug assurance that you are indeed a know-it-all.

First and foremost, because *Kaze Hikaru* is a period story, we kept all character names in their traditional Japanese form—that is, family name followed by first name. For example, the character Okita Soji's family name is Okita and his personal name is Soji.

AKO-ROSHI:

The ronin (samurai) of Ako; featured in the immortal Kabuki play *Chushingura* (Loyalty), aka *47 Samurai*.

ANI-UE:

Literally, "brother above"; an honorific for an elder male sibling.

BAKUFU:

Literally, "tent government." It is the shogunate—the feudal, military government that dominated Japan for more than 200 years.

BUSHI:

A samurai or warrior (part of the compound word *bushido*, which means "way of the samurai").

CHICHI-UE:

An honorific meaning "father above."

DO:

In kendo (a Japanese fencing sport that uses bamboo swords), this is a short way of describing the offensive single-hit strike to the stomach.

-HAN:

The same as the honorific -SAN, pronounced in the dialect of southern Japan.

-KUN:

An honorific suffix that indicates a difference in rank and title. The use of *kun* is also a way of indicating familiarity and friendliness between students or compatriots.

MEN:

In the context of *Kaze Hikaru, men* refers to one of the "points" in kendo. It is a strike to the forehead and is considered a basic move.

MIBU-ROSHI:

A group of warriors who support the Bakufu.

NE'E-SAN:

Can mean "older sister," "ma'am," or "miss."

NI'I-CHAN:

Short for oni'isan or oni'i-chan, meaning older brother.

OKU-SAMA:

This is a polite way to refer to someone's wife. *Oku* means "deep" or "further back," and comes from the fact that wives (in affluent families) stayed hidden away in the back rooms of the house.

ONI:

Literally means "ogre." This is Sei's nickname for Vice Captain Hijikata.

RANPO:

Medical science derived from the Dutch.

RONIN:
Masterless samurai.

RYO:
At the time, one *ryo* and two *bu* (four *bu* equaled roughly one *ryo*) were enough currency to support a family of five for an entire month.

-SAN:
An honorific suffix that carries the meaning of "Mr." or "Ms."

SENSEI:
A teacher, master or instructor.

SEPPUKU:
A ritualistic suicide by disembowlment that was considered a privilege of the nobility and samurai elite.

SONJO-HA:
Those loyal to the emperor and dedicated to the expulsion of foreigners from the country.

TAMEBO:
A short version of the name Tamesaburo.

YUBO:
A short version of the name Yunosuke.

Taeko Watanabe debuted as a manga artist in 1979 with her story *Waka-chan no Netsuai Jidai* (Love Struck Days of Waka). *Kaze Hikaru* is her longest-running series, but she has created a number of other popular series. Watanabe is a two-time winner of the prestigious Shogakukan Manga Award in the girls category—her manga *Hajime-chan ga Ichiban!* (Hajime-chan Is Number One!) claimed the award in 1991 and *Kaze Hikaru* took it in 2003.

Watanabe read hundreds of historical sources to create *Kaze Hikaru.* She is from Tokyo.

KAZE HIKARU VOL. 3
The Shojo Beat Manga Edition

This graphic novel contains material that was originally published in English in *Shojo Beat* magazine, May 2006–September 2006 issues.

STORY AND ART BY
TAEKO WATANABE

English Adaptation/Annette Garcia
Translation/Mai Ihara
Touch-up Art & Lettering/Gia Cam Luc
Design/Courtney Utt
Editor/Nancy Thistlethwaite

Managing Editor/Megan Bates
Editorial Director/Elizabeth Kawasaki
VP & Editor in Chief/Yumi Hoashi
Sr. Director of Acquisitions/Rika Inouye
Sr. VP of Marketing/Liza Coppola
Exec. VP of Sales & Marketing/John Easum
Publisher/Hyoe Narita

Printed in Canada

Published by VIZ Media, LLC.
P.O. Box 77010
San Francisco, CA 94107

Shojo Beat Manga Edition
10 9 8 7 6 5 4 3 2 1
First printing, November 2006

www.viz.com

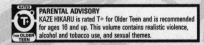

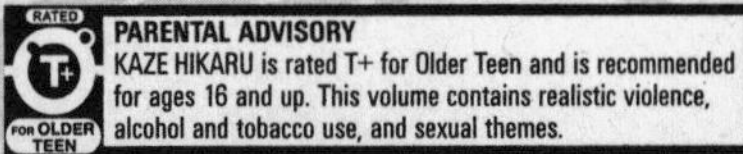

store.viz.com